BEING STILL
ABIDING IN YAHWEH

NANCY A. HEAPS

Copyright © 2016 Nancy A. Heaps

Being Still: Abiding in Yahweh
By Nancy A. Heaps
Printed in the United States of America

ISBN: 1977983472
ISBN-13: 978-1977983473

All rights reserved solely by the author. To the best of the author's knowledge, all contents are original and do not infringe upon the legal rights of any other person or work. No part of this book may be reproduced in any form without the permission of the author. The views expressed in this book are of the author alone and should not be taken as expert instruction or commands. The reader is responsible for his or her own actions. The author and the publisher do not assume any responsibility or liability whatsoever on the behalf of the purchaser or reader of these materials.

Scripture is taken from the New King James Version®. Copyright © 1982 by Thomas Nelson. Used by permission. All rights reserved.

All mentions of and quotes by Rob Stoppard are used by permission.

DEDICATION

I dedicate this book to my best Friend Jesus, my Heavenly Father Yahweh, and my Comforter Holy Spirit. I also dedicate this book in memory of Nick, my son-in-law. He may have lost his battle with mental illness, but he now resides in peace with Yahweh.

ACKNOWLEDGMENTS

I thank Terry, my husband, who stood beside me in the most difficult year of my life. Yahweh has used our marriage to teach, sharpen, and even heal us in multiple ways. What a journey it has been. I thank Rob Stoppard (of Destiny Unlimited International), who has encouraged and inspired me more than he knows. I thank Joy for being my friend and sharing her challenges and successes with me. Last but not least, I thank my daughters, Lindsey and Angelica. They, along with their children, are such a wonderful blessing to my life!

CONTENTS

1 - Introduction
5 - Little Foxes
13 - Garden Promises
19 - What Are You Looking For
25 - Favor
31 - Return to Gethsemane
35 - Trees
39 - Round Two
47 - Reflection
51 - A Dark Valley
57 - Diving Deeper
61 - Yahweh's Gifts
65 - Secret of Contentment
73 - Samson
79 - Covering
87 - Nicodemus
95 - The Heart's Condition
99 - Noodle Stick Prayers
103 - It Is Finished
107 - Prophesy
111 - The Darkest Valley
119 - Grief's Anger
123 - Gratitude
127 - Little Boats
133 - Valley Of Elah
141 - Jesus Carries Us
145 - Grace
149 - New Life
153 - Last Call
157 - Character and Integrity
161 - Vision
165- Bugged
169 - Thanksgiving
173 - Pigeon Forge
179 – Roots and Fruit
181 – Seed and Soil
185 - New Year, New Season

INTRODUCTION

In my previous book "Becoming Still, A Journey With Yahweh," I shared stories of how Yahweh (*the personal Name for God*) proved Himself to me. He showed me that He really is real. He does care about every detail of our lives. And He proved to me that each person is here for a specific purpose.

When I first began to write this book, I didn't quite know the direction it would take. Maybe I'd write individual stories as in my last book. Or maybe it'd all sort of mesh together into one large story. All I could do was take pen to paper and watch what Holy Spirit would do. I can't take credit for the writing or the story - I am simply a pen in my Father's hands.

"Being Still, Abiding in Yahweh" is a book filled with more lessons learned and true-life stories from the year 2016. Early in the year, a pastor declared it "the year of sweet 16 and the year we go 'all in' with God." Well, he missed the mark because 2016 was anything but sweet!

2016 was a year that I was 'pushed' to be all in with Yahweh. I needed Him desperately. He taught me many valuable lessons in some really hard, harsh places. I hope I can show you, the reader of these stories, how: Yahweh is Sovereign, Jesus walks beside us, and Holy Spirit comforts and guides us. Certainly, I could not have navigated the year without the Lord.

Throughout the journey, I am grateful I could abide in Yahweh – even though there were times I wasn't so sure of that fact. Abide (from the original Greek) means (in part) to stay (in a given place, state, relation or expectancy): - abide, continue, dwell, endure, be present, remain, stand, tarry (for) [1]. For me, it means a place of rest (trust), a place where I am consistently aware of the Lord's Presence in my life. It's also where I know without a shadow of doubt that Yahweh is working all things out to the good for me and those around me. To abide is to be still, but it doesn't mean "to do nothing." It's a state of being while trusting in Yahweh.

2016 started out with many physical issues which continued throughout the year. It seemed a constant battle of pain, sickness, trials, and tribulations. Issue after issue and doctor after doctor led to very few answers and very little understanding. Why must the body suffer thus affecting the soul and the spirit? I (still) haven't figured out exactly how Yahweh works. But even amid the suffering, He had much to teach me. He continued to make the connections that only He can make. Sometimes He leaves a bread-crumb trail of sorts. Other times events happened, and I was left scratching my head and unable to see what He was up to. Many times, I wished He had just spoken plainly. Sometimes He does. Yet He knows I like to treasure hunt and am intrigued by His way of doing things.

My prayer is that as you traverse my story of 2016, you will see the amazing things Yahweh accomplished. May you see how Yahweh, Jesus, Holy Spirit operate in your life as well. May you be encouraged during your storm or dark valley.

Take note: whenever you read "Yahweh" or "Holy Spirit" or "Jesus," know that I could be referring to all of Them at the same time. Sometimes I also use the terms: Abba, Daddy or Lord.

NOTE

[1] G3306 - menō - Strong's Greek Lexicon (KJV). Retrieved from https://www.blueletterbible.org//lang/Lexicon/Lexicon.cfm?Strongs=G3306&t=KJV

LITTLE FOXES

Looking at my journal, I noticed many entries where I'd written about how little things were frustrating me. For at least eight months, pain and burning in my thighs overwhelmed me, and leg aches kept me awake at night. Recently, just as I laid down, I heard the word "inflammation." By 'heard' I don't mean an audible voice spoke to me. Rather it was Holy Spirit's voice speaking inside of me. That small spoken word seemed to be a 'little thing' - a still small voice. Oh my, I tend to think everything is a little thing. Everything matters to Yahweh.

"Little" things matter whether you are talking about good or bad. I've heard many times to be careful what you listen to and what you watch as the eyes and ears are entryways into the soul and spirit. It's the little foxes that destroy the vine. Okay - exactly what does that mean? I want to see how this saying applies to my life and the process I am in right here, right now. What are the little foxes and what are they destroying?

Anything that hinders (or what we think hinders) our connection to Yahweh must be dealt with swiftly. If we see a 'giant' coming after us, we could choose to run or to stand and fight. If we stand ready for battle, we can fight full force.

When little foxes creep in, we tend to barely notice (if we see them at all). How do we miss noticing the little foxes? We might think they can't harm us. Maybe we are too distracted to notice them. It could be we are too lazy to deal with them. A little fox can greatly impact our lives or relationships (with others and with Jesus).

To show you what I mean, let me start by considering the fox in the 'natural' sense. A fox is very crafty, and its greatest weapon is to remain unseen. I think of the term 'fox in the henhouse.' It will chew, dig, and squeeze its way into the house. It is quite determined. The goal of the fox is to get in, steal eggs, kill the chickens, and get out as swiftly as possible. What defense does a chicken have? It can make a lot of noise. It can flap its wings and use its claws to scratch. It's even better if a rooster is in the house, as it will fight to the death to defend its brood. The entire commotion can wake up the farmer who then can confront the fox with greater force. Afterwards, do the chickens remember the experience? Do they remain fearful and unsure of their security? Will they remain on high alert for the next attack even if the farmer killed the fox?

I found more tidbits when I researched the habit of foxes. They adapt to almost any climate or environment. They will eat almost anything (they are not picky). They sleep during the day (light) and hunt at night (dark). They dig burrows, which are used mainly for their young. They are lone hunters with a keen sense of smell and hearing. They mark their territory with their scent to ward off other animals. They use the scent as a guide to find their way back home. They are sneaky, crafty, thieving, and cunning. This sure sounds like an enemy to me.

Once an enemy 'fox' has entered our house (body, territory, relationship, or atmosphere), it's nearly impossible to catch. And oh, the damage it can do!

Our best option is to be proactive – we can EXPECT the little fox.

We know full well that Foxy Smoxy is going to attempt a break-in. It will try to kill, steal, destroy, and devour all it can. Still, some may think Foxy is cute or harmless. WRONG – this line of thinking makes it even more dangerous. Thinking that way will cause you to let down your guard. In the spiritual realm, the "fox" is the enemy and can come in a variety of forms. It can enter relationships often unseen or undetected at first. It can chew at trust, confidence, safety, and security.

Let's use the example of a marriage and if the spouse has an affair. Surely the affair is bigger than a fox - it's more like the giant. This giant is clearly seen, and the person cheated on can gear up for war or run for cover. But what of the little foxes that precipitated the giant? One example is the times neither spouse shared or discussed their heart's concerns. Other examples may be the not-so-innocent flirtation or the little manners we don't use. Failure to grant grace, love, or mercy can cause others harm. Every little moment a spouse fails to show appreciation or when we take our loved one for granted are 'little' foxes. You may think the aforementioned little foxes seem harmless. However, Jesus said if you lust in your heart, it's the same as committing adultery - Matthew 5:27-28.

Let's look at another example - suppose a person has developed health issues. The giant is easy to spot: cancer, heart attack, clinical depression, addiction, etc. However, maybe some didn't notice the little foxes that crept in beforehand. Many may tend to put a low priority on eating healthy, working out, eliminating or reducing stress, and taking vacations. The little foxes build up in the body and eventually will manifest physically – sometimes as a giant. The more little foxes there are, the bigger the giant can become. I certainly have seen (in hindsight) the damage little foxes can do. Once you have fought a giant, you think you'd be more alert for the little foxes. I still struggle with these problems. How does someone combat these little critters before they become giants? The action we must take is not once and done (I wish it were that easy). Our action must be continual, and we must remain on watch. Our actions are not just defensive but also must be offensive.

You may wonder how this relates to temptation. If faced with a giant temptation such as murder, stealing, abuse, or robbing a bank, most would refrain from these. Consider the little fox temptations such as a 'white' lie or gossip. There's also the opportunity to offend someone or to be offended by someone. The temptation to speak harshly to a loved one is also a little fox. When you give in to these temptations, I hope you can realize what's <u>really</u> going on. You have come face to face with Foxy Smoxy! Let me assure you, you can prepare yourself with a battle plan along with the gear needed to fight the little foxes. Preparation begins within each of us. The Bible tells us to guard our hearts – Proverbs 4:23. We must be careful what we allow into our hearts and what are we exposing it to.

Take a good look at Ephesians 6:11-17 which explains the whole armor of Yahweh. Foremost, we need to realize we are strong in the Lord, in the strength of <u>His</u> might. Alone we are like helpless sheep. With Christ Jesus, we are more than conquerors (we have overwhelming victory) - Romans 8:37. Remember, we fight not against flesh and blood; ours is a spiritual battle against a host of enemies in the world and Heavenly realm – Ephesians 6:12. Back to the armor...

We put the armor on <u>ourselves</u> (not others). It is not our job to argue, offend, or attack someone else. While we can speak the truth <u>in love;</u> love must always be at the center of our interactions with others. But we can't do this alone. Alone, we fall short of the glory of Yahweh. Jesus is the One Who makes us righteous - 1 Corinthians 1:30. If someone must go around gloating about how many King James Scriptures they've memorized, they are missing the mark. Oh boy, don't even get me started on the versions of the Bible - Scripture wasn't originally written in the versions we have today (i.e., King James, New Living Translation, English Standard, etcetera). Glean what you can from the version you enjoy but do yourself a favor and check out the original text and meanings sometimes. Most importantly, don't thump someone with your favorite version.

We should desire to walk in peace - allow this gift of Holy Spirit to fill you and spill onto others. We can rest in the faith Yahweh has placed in us. Whenever troubles come (and they will) let faith rise and shield you from the enemy's attack. Our minds are protected by our salvation assurance. The enemy's favorite battleground is the mind. He will try to bring doubt, but we can always return our minds to the work of the cross. Our defensive weapon is the Sword - the Word of Yahweh. It cuts to pieces all strongholds, arguments, and thoughts contrary to Yahweh's Word. We do not use the Sword to cut someone else to pieces.

We can pray in the Spirit at all times and in every situation. We need to remain alert and be persistent in praying for others. Yet, we must remember - it is not our job to point out the splinter in someone's eye especially while we have a log in our own eye - Matthew 7:3-5, Luke 6:41-42.

The battles with the foxes and the giants are very real. Battles occur in the spiritual realm but affect the natural realm too. The battle begins with the Lord - He is all mighty and knows all things.

When we have an issue that must be dealt with, we must allow Holy Spirit to do His work. He knows best how to deal with the little foxes and the great big giants.

"Little Foxes" was originally written early in the year of 2016. In the middle of 2017, I read the story to my friend Joy... well, I tried to read it. Wouldn't you know that Yahweh 'just so happened' at that precise moment to take us through a life application of the story. Let me share....

Joy and I were at the river. It was too hot for the season, but a breeze was gently blowing thus it was rather nice in the shade. We talked and 'visited a spell' as my mom used to say. We talked of many things to include a few of our struggles and our dreams of traveling. Then I began to read "Little Foxes" to her. Before I even got half way through, an acquaintance of hers pulled up on his motorcycle. He politely asked if he could join us. It should have been obvious that I was reading aloud. I do speak softly, so maybe he didn't realize what was happening. He sat up his chair and started talking to Joy about fishing. I felt like I had suddenly become invisible! I tried reading again and again. But he was determined to talk about other things. He led the conversation with Joy to how he used to drink and how he now goes to church, then to how many heroin deaths there have been lately. I finally just laid my book down and listened to the conversation.

Then another man came over and started talking to the first guy. I thought about trying to read the story again; I really wanted to. And Joy really wanted to hear the story. It took a little while, but Joy finally spoke up - she told them that we had to leave soon and wanted to finish what we were doing before they'd arrived. Do you think those little foxes got the hint? Not right away - it took a few minutes - them talking loudly and me talking softly. Joy and I got the giggles a number of times because they just didn't seem to get it. At last, they walked away and soon left the area.

Once they were gone, Joy and I realized what Yahweh had done. We'd been given a very real opportunity to see two 'little foxes' who tried to spoil the vine. We talked about the lesson and how we can handle future opportunities. It's not really about the 'interruption' as it is what shall we do about it. I surmise that in the past, neither one of us have been bold or stood our ground. We both have gone with the 'flow' of what others (mainly the men in our lives) wanted.

We agreed that we don't need to (and should not) people please. We want to please Yahweh and do what He is doing. As we move forth in this spiritual journey, we are allowed to say 'no.' We are allowed to speak the truth in love. We did realize the battle wasn't with those two foxes. The real battle is with the enemy who wanted to disrupt what we were doing. We don't have to be manipulated or controlled by the enemy. We can take dominion over our spiritual atmosphere. We can walk in the freedom Christ has already provided. Freedom! Amazing - we can take risks and trust Holy Spirit's lead. The only One we bow down to is Yahweh, our King and Father!

GARDEN PROMISES

Mid-January through February 2016 my body continued (from the year before) to suffer with physical pain. Not only did I have to deal with the constant tingling, burning, and aching of my legs, I often felt queasy and I had headaches almost every day. If this wasn't bad enough, I felt disconnected from Yahweh. I hated feeling that way more than I hated the physical symptoms. I faced several small conflicts with my husband, Terry, which caused more stress. However, in the midst of all of this, Yahweh did some amazing things to help me see Him again.

Throughout January, my gut/stomach issues became worse. My doctor prescribed a medication for diverticulitis, but it was one that wasn't very helpful for that condition. The problem continued throughout February. At the beginning of March, the doctor prescribed the same unhelpful medication. I don't understand why Doctors don't listen or pay closer attention. The diverticulitis progressed and forced me to go into the hospital in the middle of March. I was very seriously ill, and I received intensive IV antibiotics. It took a day or two before I started to feel better. It's interesting that while I was in the hospital, the pain (and burning) in my legs was minor.

While all of this had been going on, I questioned (and regretted) the purchase of my travel trailer. When I first purchased it, I'd planned on living in it. However, due to a series of events, that idea became unrealistic. I began to doubt my ability to make the 'right' decision. I even called myself stupid, and I even beat myself up over that decision. Furthermore, I didn't understand Terry, how he processes life's concerns, or why we were going through these events. My life coach, Rob Stoppard, explained that I was holding a "judgment" which occurs when we hold something against ourselves or another person. That, in turn, will cause us to build a spiritual wall of sorts between us and others. Any wall we build between us and Yahweh is really a fabrication of our own mind. Yahweh doesn't see a wall, and He will never leave nor forsake us. However, we cannot see clearly with this block wall in the way.

Around the same time all these issues were going on, someone gave me a prophetic word. I was told: "You are like a screen door that acts like a filter. Holy Spirit can flow through you onto others." Later, Rob told me "a screen door sometimes gets flies and other bugs on it causing a disruption in the flow of air. You need to turn around at times and allow Holy Spirit to clean the screen/filter." Maybe I took on too much and needed some time alone with the Lord to heal….

In spite of the issues, Holy Spirit continued to teach me in various ways: via Scripture, sermons, messages, and very real-life lessons (in my life and the lives of others). He led me through the book of Hosea and helped me to see the story from a perspective different from how I previously viewed it. In the past, I'd been able to somewhat imagine the story from Hosea's and Yahweh's viewpoint. This time I saw it through the prostitute's eyes.

Weren't all of us "the prostitute" at one time or another? This may not be literally true (in this natural realm) but is most likely true spiritually.

Gomar used her body and seductive skills to survive. Maybe that is all she knew. She earned a living selling what was meant to be precious between a husband and wife. She must have been a good actress. I can't imagine she actually enjoyed that lifestyle. When love doesn't exist or if no substantial connection occurs between two people, sex becomes meaningless or even possibly degrading. In the book of Hosea, the prostitute represented Israel, her idolatry and harlotry, and her separation and disconnection from Yahweh. Let's see how this story applies to the church (the individual believer)...

Keep in mind that Yahweh, Holy Spirit, Jesus are Three but also One. They are One within us as Holy Spirit dwells in each believer. It's hard to imagine – wherever we go and whatever we do - They are with us in that place and in that action. I believe Yahweh has always wanted us to see ourselves fully connected to Him. And He desires for us to live in abundant relationship with Him, just as He did with Adam and Eve before the fall. They had a simple choice to make: tree of life or tree of knowledge of good and evil. Even after they sinned (missed the mark), Yahweh never left them. However, they struggled to see this truth. We have the same choice - life in the spirit with Jesus or not? Spirit realm or natural realm?

The promise is hidden in the problem. Say what – what does that mean? Ok, let me see if I can figure this one out by breaking it down. What is the promise and what is the problem?

Well, the enemy brings the problems. The enemy is a thief, destroyer, and killer - John 10:10a. He prowls around like a lion looking for someone to devour - 1 Peter 5:8. HOWEVER, Jesus destroyed the devil's work; Jesus rendered the devil powerless - 1 John 3:8, Hebrews 2:14-15.

We have been rescued from the domain of darkness and transferred into the Kingdom - Colossians 1:13. Nothing can separate us from Yahweh's love which is in Christ Jesus our Lord - Romans 8:38-39.

What promises did Adam and Eve have or carry? They were (we are) created in the image of Yahweh, as we all have three parts: Spirit, Body, and Soul (the soul being: mind, will, emotions). Adam and Eve were given dominion over the earth and the animals within it. Yahweh blessed them, and they could procreate – have children and produce the fruit of the land. They could fill the earth and subdue it. They were given food and had all they needed to sustain life. Adam was given work: to tend and keep the garden. Eve was created from Adam's rib and intended to be his helper (but not less than him). They became one flesh (intimately and emotionally). They were naked and had no shame. They had an open and free relationship with Yahweh and with each other.

Okay, what was the problem in the garden? Adam and Eve had a choice and used their free will to listen to and believe the enemy instead of Yahweh. The enemy caused them to question Yahweh's promise, provision, and goodness. Satan deceived Eve by attacking her identity. It started with his questions – "Did God actually say…?" Eve (and Adam) knew exactly what Yahweh had said. Then satan lied "you will surely not die…" Was he speaking of the spiritual, natural, or both? Then another lie was told – "your eyes will be opened, and you will be like God" (Genesis 3:5 NKJV). Silly serpent, Yahweh already had made them in His image (like Him) - Genesis 1:26-27.

Adam and Eve acted on the lie of the enemy by eating of the tree of knowledge of good and evil. THEN their eyes were opened to their nakedness (literally and spiritually). They saw themselves separated from Yahweh and they tried to hide from Him. Of course, He knew where they were the entire time. A simple lie caused them to feel shame, which led to blame and disconnection.

I believe I am already fully restored to Yahweh. It amazes me that even before I was born into this earth, Yahweh had made a way back to Himself via Jesus. Wow, look how Yahweh used marriage (between Adam & Eve and Hosea & Gomar) to show me His promise. Within a marriage, one can experience a physical, emotional, and spiritual connection.

So... what was the real (deep rooted) problem I had at that point in time? I've struggled (most of my life) with relationships and the ability to receive love – to believe a man's love is true and honest. My past was deplete of healthy expressions of real love. At times, I thought I'd be better off alone. But if left alone, people can't give or receive pure love.

Within my marriage, if Terry and I are divided, we can't stand. We must be on the 'same page' or as the Bible calls it 'equally yoked.' Contention, strife, arguing, and fighting are not exhibitions of Yahweh's true nature or His image, likeness, character, and integrity. Mistrust, broken promises, and unwillingness to fully yield or commit leads down a rocky road. Iron sharpens iron and a friend really does sharpen a friend - Proverbs 27:17.

If Terry and I work through the battles as a unit, we will be stronger. Instead of fighting with each other, we should team up and fight the problems. Unfortunately, most people's 'natural' instinct is to battle the one they see standing in front of them. Marriage was created by Yahweh to provide many benefits.

Working through the challenges together, we will fully experience Yahweh's covenant. His great love and full acceptance are deep within our hearts because He dwells there.

Hidden within Terry's and my relationship is the ability to express this same love and acceptance to one another. Jesus already paid the full price, and we don't have to strive to achieve what was already finished. He already has restored, redeemed, and healed. His agape love is an ever-flowing river full of life which fills us to overflowing. We are free as He set us free before we even existed in this natural realm. We are in the garden of Yahweh's Presence.

WHAT ARE YOU LOOKING FOR

I can't tell you how many times I've walked into a room and forgot what I'd been looking for. I'll stand there dumbfounded trying to bring my reason for being there back into my mind. Eventually, I will give up, sit back down, get comfortable, and poof the item I'd needed pops back into my head. I am sure many other people have this same experience. This could be a sign of one's age or perhaps it's just absent-mindedness.

How often do we forget to pay attention to our spiritual well-being? How often do we look, but we do not see? Certainly, more things are going on in the spiritual realm than in this natural realm. I've read the Bible several times, yet it seems each time I read, I find verses that seem to 'jump off the page.' I find it interesting because I see or learn something new all the time. The Word really is alive. Let me share what I recently discovered, starting with Mark 11:11…

Jesus went into Jerusalem and into the Temple. He looked around at all things, but because it was late in the day, He left and went to Bethany with the twelve disciples. Notice the hour was late; it's possible that no one was in or around the Temple. What was He looking at? Was He observing the activity in the spiritual realm? Was He foreseeing what would occur the following day? Maybe He was remembering what the Scriptures said about the Temple.

The very next day Jesus and His disciples left Bethany and Jesus was hungry. He saw a fig tree with leaves but no fruit. Jesus spoke to the tree saying, "let no one eat fruit from you ever again." I found this quite odd as it was too early in the season for fruit. (See Mark 11:12-14.) Why then was Jesus expecting to find figs?

After the fruitless fig tree was cursed, Jesus and His disciples went back to Jerusalem. Jesus entered the Temple (again) and drove out the money changers. Jesus then said "Is it not written, My house shall be called a house of prayer for all nations? But you have made it a den of thieves." (Mark 11:17 NKJV). He was referencing Isaiah 56:7 and Jeremiah 7:11.

Why was Jesus angry? Well, the money changers and dove sellers were ripping people off. The money changers exchanged foreign currency for their country's currency, but they charged high exchange rates. "Foreign currency" represents foreign gods or idols – things that mean <u>nothing</u> in Yahweh's Kingdom. Today, do people exchange the Kingdom currency for meaningless rituals or trinkets? Yahweh's Kingdom currency is love, faith, grace, and mercy. "...Faith is the substance of things hoped for, the evidence of things not seen" (Hebrews 11:1 NJKV). Yahweh utilizes Kingdom currency to create what we hope and ask for – when we and our requests align with His perfect will.

After the Temple was cleared, later that evening, Jesus and the disciples left the city. Peter told Jesus to LOOK; the cursed fig tree had withered. Jesus answered - have faith in God (Father, Son, Holy Spirit) [1]. He said if we believe and don't doubt, we can move mountains. When we ask in prayer for anything, we must believe, and we will receive. However, we come in prayer first, forgiving others so the Father may likewise forgive us. If we hold something against another person, <u>we</u> are the ones in bondage. If we harbor unforgiveness, the Father won't forgive us – Mark 11:25-26. What we bind on earth is bound in Heaven. What we loose on earth is loosed in Heaven. Let's not hang onto grudges or hold something against another person. If we do, we might be the one left bound.

Just as Jesus observed the spiritual activity in the Temple that first night, He observes the spiritual activity in the temple of our hearts. What does He see? Are we like the fruitless fig tree – unproductive? We should produce good fruit, but we aren't able to do this on our own. Connected to Jesus (the Vine), we have His Life's blood (sap) running through our veins. Will you live with Him or will you wither and die? Let us be ready in season and out of season - 2 Timothy 4:2! Let's freely give what we have received.

Unfortunately, there still are 'money changers' today. They cheat others when they don't share love, joy, peace, patience, kindness, goodness, and so on. Who or what is FIRST in your heart – Yahweh or idols (money, material things, prestige…)? I encourage you to allow Holy Spirit to drive out the distractions which cause you to lose awareness of Yahweh.

Often the way we see things in the natural is upside down from how it really is in Yahweh's Kingdom. No matter how hard we try, we can't change the condition of our hearts by ourselves. Jesus turned the tables on the money changers – Mark 11:15. He can also turn the tables in our hearts. We need to give Him free access.

Furthermore, it's very important to realize that Yahweh has never left us. Many don't see Him or His activity in their lives. Many have disqualified themselves; they see themselves as 'least.' They cannot recognize their true value. The truth is, ALL of us are great in Yahweh's eyes, simply because He treasures everyone.

Jesus didn't stop with the money changers; He also overturned the seats of the dove sellers. The word "seat" is the exalted seat of high ranking men (teachers, judges and such). Doves were important as they were offered as a sacrifice by women after childbirth, cleansed lepers, those healed of bodily discharges, and those who couldn't afford more expensive sacrifices. Furthermore, Holy Spirit descended like a dove when Jesus was baptized – Matthew 3:16, Mark 1:10, Luke 3:22, John 1:32.

The dove sellers sold doves at exuberant rates. They took advantage of the poor and sick. The 'dove sellers' today are the religious leaders who 'sell' Holy Spirit for a price. That's just wrong! Holy Spirit is free to everyone; we all have free access. His work includes healing, cleansing, and bringing us into relationship with Yahweh. Just as Jesus overturned the seats of the dove sellers, He will overturn the seat in our hearts. What seat? The place within our heart that is often ruled by the flesh, old wounds, or the evil one. The first step is to realize that we can't fix ourselves. We need to surrender all our junk and submit our whole hearts (all of who we are) to Christ.

Jesus continued His work by not allowing anyone to carry wares through the Temple - Mark 11:16. The Temple was not to be used as a marketplace. Furthermore, using the Temple as a thoroughfare or shortcut was an inappropriate use of the Temple. Wares are: a vessel, implement (household utensil, domestic gear, tackle and armament of vessels, specifically sails and ropes). Metaphorically for body (souls live temporarily in bodies) - - a) men of quality a chosen instrument. b) in a bad sense, an assistant in accomplishing an evil deed. ²

Now, what wares do we try to carry through the Temple (keeping in mind we are the temple of Holy Spirit)? Wares are anything we cling to which hinders His work inside of us. Wares can be doubt, unbelief, unforgiveness, judgment, malice, hatred, religious acts (instead of relationship with Yahweh), and so on. Allowing ourselves to be a marketplace and 'sell' the wrong ideals is inappropriate. If we are doing such things, we are cheating others from experiencing Yahweh's true Kingdom.

Jesus' anger was justified as the money changers and dove sellers made the Temple into a den of thieves. The ultimate thief is satan and his demonic forces. It's ironic that Jesus was treated like a thief, arrested, and killed beside two other thieves. However, Jesus was NOT common, and He was not a thief!

Okay, let me connect the dots and see if a picture forms…

The churches in Revelation chapters 2 and 3 were actual churches. But what is written to them also applies to the entire church (individual believers and the entire body). Look closely at what Jesus said to the church in Laodicea, specifically Revelation 3:17. People who think they are rich (having material wealth), are instead spiritually wretched, miserable, poor, blind, and naked. They are lukewarm – kind of 'middle of the road.' They aren't fully on fire for Yahweh nor are they fully against Him.

The Temple was supposed to be a place of prayer. It was not designed or created to be used for idol/self-worship. Since the believer is the temple of Holy Spirit, we have and can exhibit His fruit and His gifts. We freely give (share) what we have freely received. The believer is designed to be a place of prayer, which involves real relationship with Yahweh.

Religious people don't produce good fruit, just as the fig tree didn't produce fruit. Religious people tend to misappropriate the temple (using people for their own sordid purposes). They tend to 'worship' themselves or idols (money, material things, etc.). They aren't really interested in worshiping the Lord. They aren't concerned about a real relationship with Him. And they probably aren't even familiar with Yahweh's Kingdom or His currency.

I have said before that I detest religion. Instead, I desire a relationship with Yahweh. I ask Holy Spirit to turn the tables on anything that tries to hinder my relationship with Yahweh. Oh my, I'm sure this will involve some process. As I walk this out, I will be watchful, and I shall pay attention to what I see.

NOTES

[1] G2316 - theos - Strong's Greek Lexicon (KJV). Retrieved from https://www.blueletterbible.org//lang/Lexicon/Lexicon.cfm?Strongs=G2316&t=KJV

[2] G4632 - skeuos - Strong's Greek Lexicon (KJV). Retrieved from https://www.blueletterbible.org//lang/Lexicon/Lexicon.cfm?Strongs=G4632&t=KJV

FAVOR

Early in the year of 2016, I struggled with not feeling favored and noticed many instances where this seemed to be a reality in my life. I think my problem was: 1) somehow my ear had been tuned to the enemy's voice instead of Yahweh's. 2) I was looking at the negative side of my circumstances instead of what Yahweh was doing. 3) It seemed I'd lost track of what Yahweh's Word says about me and my life.

After about eight months of health issues, that 3-fold problem had become my main focus. The cause of my health issues remained a mystery to me throughout the entire year. I suffered with these very natural physical feelings, along with my soulish emotions. My mind often returned to my past and the number of instances that I'd been ill and even close to death. At times, I even despaired of my very life; I wanted to be free of this body. I wanted to leave this world and return in full to the Father. I felt bad about feeling that way, and guilt/shame were my hosts.

The enemy hissed his lies and insinuations (just as he has since the beginning of earth time): 1) Where is God? 2) Why isn't He healing you? 3) What have you done to deserve this? The last question carried triple edge lies - A) you are guilty and condemned and won't ever get it right. B) God is chastising you for no reason. C) you don't deserve this; therefore, God is mean.

To my dismay, I either entertained those questions and thoughts or I just simply ignored them! Only the truth can combat a lie, and only Holy Spirit's Light can dispel darkness. The enemy will attack us at our core. He wants to destroy our very identity. He tries to make us believe the lie that we are disconnected or separated from the Father. The longer we stay in the pit (of defeat, depression, anger, and so on), the more the enemy dumps condemnation on us. It is a horrible place to be and it's <u>not</u> where Yahweh meant for us to go (even if it is only in our mind). I admit I got lost and buried in that pit way too often. I looked too closely at a present circumstance, heaped on past circumstances, and began to believe the lies that this is how it would always be - AND that somehow it is what I deserved.

Sometimes I tend to think it's hard to redirect my thoughts while my flesh and soul want for some sick reason to stay in the pit. Probably because it is familiar, it gives an excuse not to move forward, and I really don't realize renewal of the mind must occur. Haven't I yet realized that it's the job of Holy Spirit to renew and heal! It's best to nip the enemy's lies in the bud – speak the Truth of Yahweh's Word. Once again, I must allow the tables to be turned.   I must relinquish control and allow Him to do what only He can do! What is my part then. I simply run to Jesus, direct my attention to Him, and what He's already done. I invite Holy Spirit to do His work deep inside of me.

Oh brother - I admit I was throwing myself a grand pity party that no one else would attend. I kept seeing the illnesses – the many times I'd been in the battle and how it had become exponentially worse. I used to have only one issue to deal with at a time. It was usually clear cut what the problem was. For example, maybe I had an ear infection or maybe a migraine. Then one became two problems at the same time. Eventually, I ended up with several health challenges, one of which no one has yet been able to define clearly. I've been in the illness storms again and again and again. And each time I'd see all the storms (present and past). I somehow lumped them all together, and it seemed that all the storms were upon me at the same time. I'd cry out "WHY?" I shed a river of tears. I questioned, "Why isn't Yahweh healing me?"

We can't give away what we do not have. Well that statement led me into another tizzy! How can I ever do what Jesus did?! Then suddenly Holy Spirit revealed something to me. **All** (every single one) of my past health problems had been healed and resolved! Yahweh had instilled healing IN me! Healing is now a huge part of who I am (or maybe it always was, and I am just now realizing it).

The enemy had tried to compound the issues and make me believe they were all upon me at the same moment. But the Lord had removed them from me and my life every time! He reminded me that there is NO condemnation for me as I am in Christ Jesus. He already had set me free from the law of sin and death - Romans 8:1-2. I am not in the realm of the flesh, but I am in the realm of the Spirit, as indeed Holy Spirit lives in me - Romans 8:9a. He Who raised Jesus gives life to my mortal body - Romans 8:11. I am fully convinced that NOTHING can separate me from the love of Yahweh. Yahweh demonstrated His own love for me as Christ died for me, absolving me from all sin. (See Romans 5:8.)

I shall go forward; I shall choose to believe what Yahweh says instead of any circumstance, my feelings, or my own understanding. I will choose to cling to Jesus, trusting fully that

He knows all things, and He has me and this situation in His

Sovereign control.

Is it easy to walk in faith? Not when something (i.e. the soul, the enemy's lies, continuing symptoms, questions, doubt, or unbelief) gets in the way. Oh man I don't like this - I don't want to be distracted. Too often, I am not even aware of when I <u>am</u> distracted!

Let me share more about the recent attack. I had diverticulitis, and I fought it for as long as I could, mainly because I <u>hate</u> being in the hospital. I prayed and pleaded for healing. I really didn't understand Yahweh's way of doing things; He still has much to teach me. Finally, I gave in and asked Terry to drive me to the hospital.

The emergency department was bursting at the seams. It was noisy and chaotic. It seemed every seat was filled. Then I noticed one man with a serious cut that was bleeding profusely. I quickly surmised that if I remained there, my wait would run into the next day. So, I asked Terry to drive me to another hospital. It seemed he took the longest possible route to get there. I had a three hour wait in that emergency department. I was in incredible pain, even my legs ached and tingled. All I wanted was to feel better! I didn't know it yet, but Yahweh was about to show me His favor and mercy.

Finally, I was taken back to the examination room. A doctor appeared immediately and talked with me (not at me). Even though I was physically suffering, I still encouraged my first IV tech. Soon, I was given something for the pain and nausea, then taken for a CT scan. And not much later I was taken to a private room with big windows and a nice view. Every person who came into that room was pleasant, and their main objective was to ensure I received the best care.

In the past, I wanted out of the hospital as quickly as I had entered it. This time, I settled in and relaxed. I knew I was dangerously ill. I'd pushed myself to the limit. That hospital was where I needed to be, and I am very grateful for the care and attention I received. My doctor, Dr. "S", had an incredible bedside manner. Each nurse and technician performed their duties efficiently. Everyone was nice to me. It seemed one nurse was (at first) having a bad day. Then she tripped on a blanket, and I asked if she was okay. My concern for her was clear, and it seemed to lighten her mood. From that point on I joked around with her. When it was time for me to leave, she was the one who walked out with me. She told me that a new hospital is being built on the west end of town and I asked about the current building. She didn't know what they were going to do with it. I said, "it'd be cool if I could buy it and turn it into a place to help people." She told me that if do, to let her know, and she'd come and work for me. It is amazing how a simple gesture of kindness can encourage someone.

The enemy's lies might try to convince me I didn't do much or what I had done didn't really matter. The truth is love is patient and kind, and I am full of Yahweh's love. It's His love that I share with others. His steadfast love won't ever depart from me. I can simply be myself and speak what Holy Spirit gives me to speak.

While I was in the hospital, it's interesting that I didn't read the Bible, listen to sermons, or process any study. The Word is alive inside of me, and Holy Spirit is always with me. He ministered to me and blessed me. Yahweh showed me favor which I fully felt and experienced. Resting in favor is unfamiliar to me. I'm used to helping others, not receiving help. In my past, I often met other's needs out of my own need to be accepted, valued, and favored. While they may have enjoyed what I gave, I often was left feeling used, manipulated, and only loved for what I had done or given. I didn't feel loved just for ME.

I can't imagine what lies ahead. I have much to learn about Yahweh's favor. His healing work shall continue to become really real inside of me. Hopefully, revealing these things will bring the dross to the surface, and I rest in faith. I willingly lay all my concerns at the feet of Jesus. I ask Him to help me to see myself as He sees me, in every aspect. I break down every wall and barrier by the power and authority of Jesus Christ that would try to hinder His work inside me. Whatever hindered my ability to receive favor, I break that chain. May I glean great wisdom from this experience and may I share that with others along the way.

RETURN TO GETHSEMANE

Once again, I am led to the story of the garden of Gethsemane - Matthew 26:36-56, Mark 14:32-52; Luke 22:39-53, John 18:1-11. I've often wondered about that night. A few of the disciples (Peter, James, and John) were given special honor. They went with Jesus deeper into that garden. Three times they fell asleep while Jesus prayed. And three times He woke them from their snooze fest. It seems they were very sleepy. They chose sleep over obedience. What were they supposed to watch for? If they remained awake, I can only imagine what they would have seen. The Bible doesn't tell us what the other disciples were doing. Perhaps they fell asleep as well.

It's really hard to fathom. These men walked with Jesus and experienced all that Jesus did. They saw Jesus' signs, wonders, and healing miracles. They saw demons cast out of people. And they even saw how the weather obeyed Jesus' voice. They <u>knew</u> what Jesus was capable of as they were literally eye-witnesses. Furthermore, they were well trained and had served in ministry to other people. Still, on that ONE night, they slumbered and did NOT watch. Some might say it's because they weren't yet filled with Holy Spirit since that didn't happen until after Jesus was resurrected – Acts 1:4,5,8 and Acts 2:1-4.

I take a good look into the mirror of my heart. I pray I haven't fallen asleep like those men did on that dark night in the garden while the Savior prayed. I'm sure others doze at the wheel of life.

Why are many believers' are sleepy? I don't understand how this is possible. After all, we have Holy Spirit filling us! Seriously if our spirits slumber, we can't be fully aware of what's happening in the spiritual realm. Asleep we will not be on watch. We live in this time and season. Jesus has also told us to watch.

Looking for answers, I completed a word search for "watch." In the NKJV - Matthew 14:25, 24:43a; Mark 6:48; Luke 2:8, 12:38, watch means a guarding or (concretely, guard), the act, the person; figuratively, the place, the condition, or (specially), the time (as a division of day or night), literally or figuratively: - cage, hold, (im-) prison(-ment), ward, watch [1]. This word can also mean: to keep awake, i.e. watch (literally or figuratively): - be vigilant, wake, (be) watch(-ful) [2]. And finally, there is this meaning: of uncertain affinity; to abstain from wine (keep sober), i.e. (figuratively) be discreet: - be sober, watch [3].

Okay, back to that night and its details... In Luke 22:39, we learn Jesus usually went to the Mount of Olives to pray. It was His custom to go there. Ok, that night wasn't so unusual, not at the start anyway. His first warning or alert to the disciples was "pray not to enter into temptation." They were forewarned; basically, Jesus told them that temptation was coming. Temptation is always ready to pounce. They did not have to give into temptation (to NOT pray, to NOT watch, to NOT fall asleep); but they did. We don't have to give into temptation either.

Jesus walked away from the disciples to pray. For some reason, I had pictured quite a distance separated them. But Luke 22:41 shows us that He went about a stone's throw away. Hmmm, how far away was He? I can't throw a stone very far, but others might. My nephew used to play baseball and could throw 90 mph pitches. His throw could probably reach a good distance. I imagine that professional baseball players could throw even further.

That night, at that distance, was it even possible for the disciples to see or hear Jesus? They could have watched the way He petitioned the Father. Throughout just a few years they'd seen Jesus operate in many ways. He forgave, healed, delivered. He was a compassionate teacher who remained humble (meek). That fateful night, Jesus cried out to the Father and looked for the Father's will. Jesus asked if the Father was willing to take away the cup of burden (of carrying all sin and His feeling of being briefly separated from the Father). Yet Jesus submitted to the Father's will (not His own).

Those disciples, on that dark and weary night, had available to them a very intimate and meaningful encounter between Jesus and the Father. It is interesting that this occurred in Gethsemane which means oil press and while there Jesus felt the pressure of what He was about to face. Luke 22:44 tells us that Jesus was in such agony, His sweat became like large drops of blood.

I have been stressed before, but not at the point of practically sweating blood. While I was in the hospital, I was mildly stressed compared to what the Lord experienced. I hope I saw or sensed most of what Yahweh did. Certainly, I don't want to miss a thing He does or says! I hope others feel the same way. Can anyone envision what He has in store for us? My battle cry begins – wake up sleepy church!!!

NOTES

[1] G5438 - phylakē - Strong's Greek Lexicon (KJV). Retrieved from https://www.blueletterbible.org//lang/Lexicon/Lexicon.cfm?Strongs=G5438&t=KJV

[2] G1127 - grēgoreō - Strong's Greek Lexicon (KJV). Retrieved from https://www.blueletterbible.org//lang/Lexicon/Lexicon.cfm?Strongs=G1127&t=KJV

[3] G3525 - nēphō - Strong's Greek Lexicon (KJV). Retrieved from https://www.blueletterbible.org//lang/Lexicon/Lexicon.cfm?Strongs=G3525&t=KJV

TREES

Healing can take its good ole time and has forced me to become even more still. I'm very weak and tired. How I struggle with this! I don't know why, especially since this seems to be the opportune time for Holy Spirit to move. He speaks in such a small still voice. I run to Daddy and discover a place among the trees. I begin to relax in His Presence. I park my car, open my sunroof's visor, cover my legs with a blanket, put my seat back, and play worship music. The trees move and dance to the music as I softly sing along. Here I rest while I watch the trees move and I think how trees are alive.

This is my deepest heart's cry: I want to be fully in Yahweh's Presence at all times. It's a place of intimacy and extravagant worship. Holy Spirit I ask, take me into that intimate fellowship with Jesus. I long to rest my head on His chest and even put my forehead on His neck. I want to feel and hear His heartbeat, the drum, drum, drumming of Heaven's base beating in My Lord and Savior's veins. Oh, to feel the heat from His skin as His hand brushes the hair off my face. Rough and callused, His are carpenter's hands with nail print scars and all. To sense His smile and feel His love envelop me, oh how amazingly wonderful.

Lord Jesus let me remain with You! It's not that I long to be free of this world, this body, the troubles, and the worries… well, that's true somewhat I suppose. In truth, I simply long to literally be with You. I want to hear the sound of Your voice and the soft rumble of Your laughter as these pour out of You and spill onto me. You share the greatest and most amazing love. Words escape me, how can these be explained in human terms. Your love Lord is ultimately safe, pure, free, and unconditional. Nothing can compare!

I take a very deep breath, slowly releasing all tension, stress, and health issues. Calm down my soul and spirit – deeper…. deeper, peace, be still… even stiller I say. We've no place to go and no task to do. Become calm as the sea with no wind or rain. Picture the moonlight as it barely kisses the surface of the water. Perfect stillness. Breathe – and breathe again. Quiet body, spirit, soul; slow down heartbeat. Let Daddy's peace ripple over us – breathe, breathe, and deeply breathe again.

Come Holy Spirit, more … more … even more. I desire deeper communion with You. I wait here; I wait upon You Lord. I breathe You in, more, breathe and again! I am still and know You are Yahweh. Right here, right now You are with me and I with You. I treasure this quiet place of deepest intimacy. I whisper "Yahweh" and know Your Presence covers me. More Lord, more, I want more of You!!

Spirit, soul, and body of mine I say quiet…. even more quiet. I command all voices and thoughts within me to be quiet and still. I shall remain here, in this quiet space with the Lord and Savior, Jesus. How I've missed this! Life's pain, distractions, and troubles had pulled me away. But no more! Praise the Lord! I am back – near and dear to my Savior's heart. I am in the very Presence of El Elyon, the most high God!

I cherish the lovely moments - quiet and undisturbed - as I center my heart on Jesus, Yahweh, Holy Spirit. It's a wonderful place where everything else fades away. I don't have to struggle - I just need to abide in Jesus.

I left my sanctuary, returned home, wrote what I experienced, and now I ponder... Am I ready for the opportunities He has for me? Will I move past these early tests/proofs? I know not what to do. My soul is not in charge. I shall not be led by my mind, will, or emotions. I do not care if my soul understands or agrees with what I am doing. I do not care that the body struggles with pain – in the sense of allowing it to stop me from moving forward with the reason I am here. Sure, it would be easier if I didn't have to deal with the physical problems or the soul's issues. I'm tired of these waylaying me! I can't wait till I feel better (in these areas) to do what I am here for. Time is short. I must complete my task. I must take steps of faith. The Lord shall provide what I need in each place I land. The soul would like answers.

I stopped writing and 'just so happened' to watch an early episode of the show Touch. I felt a very strong urge to watch it. The word I just heard on the show was "triangulation!!" Of course, it's tied to all Yahweh does and has done. Anyway, on that episode, an astronaut said something about 3 distinct individual points connected by 5191 miles - triangulation, in this case, an isosceles triangle. Then Kiefer Sutherland said, "We can't change the past, but the future is a different story." Then the child (as narrator) said: "If two points are destined to touch, the universe will always find a way to make a connection." He said this as a woman threw a penny into a fountain and the camera zoomed into the change: nickels, dimes, pennies, and quarters. In my previous book, you'll find a story entitled "Triangulation." You'll also discover the significance of nickels, and other change within the story "Rae of Hope."

Finally, the day was done and when I laid down to sleep, I started to feel unwell; my body ached and the front of my throat at the thyroid really hurt to the touch. And I was sad. I was sad that in the deep mysteries of Yahweh I felt alone. I want Terry to share in the excitement of what I see. I want him to come alongside me in this spiritual journey. His lack of enthusiasm, attention, and awareness has tried to make me doubt what I have seen and heard. How can it be Lord that You would want me here, with Terry and in this place? I wanted to cry, hard. Yet I'm not even sure what I'd be crying about. I don't know where this emotional agony comes from. I suppose I've always had the gift (of being a seer). Perhaps I was shut off or shut up before. Others may have thought I was weird. They might have questioned my sanity. Maybe I was told I didn't see or hear what I really did. It could be people claimed the benefits or even my gift as their own.

What is the purpose of what I have experienced? I cling to the faith and the belief that Yahweh has shown me these things. But I do not know why. I certainly don't want to bury my head in the sand. I want to complete the tasks Yahweh has for me - whatever they all may be. I need guidance and encouragement, especially when life feels useless. I don't know the purpose of what He has shown me, except maybe just to get my attention. I am grateful for that. To know He is active in my life is pretty amazing.

ROUND TWO

After only a few weeks of being discharged from the hospital, I still couldn't eat or drink much, even though my stomach growled for food. What a whirlwind of frustration! I was not getting better. As a matter of fact, I ended up feeling like death warmed over. I finally gave in and went back to the hospital. A CT scan confirmed diverticulitis again! Unfortunately, they sent me home with oral antibiotics and instead of getting better, I got much worse. A few days later I called Dr. "S" and he called ahead to the emergency department, so I'd be seen quickly.

Geez, how does one get their mind off suffering and return the focus to Yahweh? I know He's not gone anywhere and neither had I. But in the pain pit, I lost some of that sense of wonder and the deep inner knowing of Holy Spirit. I know full well there has been <u>many</u> times He has healed me. I trusted that this issue would also be taken care of; I would see divine health manifest. My soul struggled with the 'why.' When I entered the hospital, I didn't know that Holy Spirit was about to do some amazing things...

Originally, I was assigned a room on the 2nd floor. It wasn't a private room, but I was alone Friday and Saturday night. Sunday, I got a roommate. Monday (seemingly out of the blue) I got moved to the 1st floor and a different person, Linda, was in that room.

At one point, Linda suddenly started coughing and couldn't catch her breath. I could feel her panic and fear. I just quietly prayed and within seconds she was fine. I relaxed and read a good bit from a book about the Christian spiritual realm. I recognized that at times I walk in that realm. The author mentioned that we can't go too long without our spirit being fed, as it will grow weak. I think it would lead the spirit to slumber or even to fall sound asleep. Hold on a second! Wow - is this a spiritual analogy of what had manifested physically in me?! Or maybe it's that I allowed my spirit to get weak and the body (natural) followed. I struggled to recall the last time I ate a real meal – in either realm. No one in the natural can force another person to eat, and Holy Spirit won't force feed us in the spiritual realm either. I had grown weak in my spirit and needed to come fully awake; only then would my body awaken and strengthen as it should. I had neglected to feed my body and my spirit, I must take full responsibility for that. I allowed my soul to take over and run amuck.

While I was reading, I realized Linda had a bubbling oxygen machine. And in that same moment, I read how the prophetic bubbles up. How cool! I read the few lines to Linda and she thought it was cool too. In order for Holy Spirit to bubble up His Word, I must get quiet and listen. I'll be able to tune in more to Him and hear what He is saying. Most times, Holy Spirit speaks very softly. I don't want to miss what He's saying just because I'm distracted. I want to walk in the spiritual realm. I want to see angels and even do miracles. I can imagine the amazing things He can do through me. I just don't know _why_ I haven't yet done the greater things. I'm not sure how to discover the greater things or how I'd even begin doing them.

As I laid 'still' in that uncomfortable hospital bed, I really was trying to give my body time to heal. My belly was somewhat irritated, but the hurt subsided after a few days. Terry visited me only a few times and stayed only a short bit each time. I understand anyone's resistance to be a visitor. I don't like either end of it (being a visitor or a patient).

Alone in my hospital bed, I realized I'd landed in the pit of despair because of the attacks on my body. My body became weak and wanted to reject my spirit so I could go 'home' (to Heaven). Too often I became distracted and became angry. I laid blame on the Lord and myself. I complained, wondered, and questioned. I felt hurt and lost even though I know Holy Spirit never left me. I couldn't understand why these things were happening to me. I even doubted I could hear the Lord's voice. Along the way, perhaps I blamed Yahweh for what was happening to my body. If I held anything against Him, I'd not fully approach Him. If I blame Him, I can't see Him as a good Father. While I know Yahweh doesn't cause illness, my mind reasoned that He IS Sovereign, and He can heal instantly. Sigh, the enemy consistently tries to plant doubt in my head. Obviously, I continually need Holy Spirit's revelation and help.

I know I've already learned I'll drive <u>toward</u> whatever I'm <u>looking at</u>? If I remain fully focused on the agony, frustration, and illness, then this is what I will see. Lord help me. My ultimate goal, my greatest need is to have a deeper relationship and connection with my Creator. If I lack this, I lack everything!

The natural things (health, wealth, material things) are valueless without the Lord. Relying on or taking advantage of one's health or belongings will lead to a dead-end street. This natural life moves on and one day it shall end – then what? We will move into spiritual life, which never ends. But while I am here, I want to be healthy and finish this 'race' well. I praise Yahweh that my attention can shift right back to Him. Okay, back to the hospital journey...

Linda's husband spent a great deal of time in the hospital with her. He really doted on her. At first, I didn't talk much with either of them. At one point, she needed a procedure done so I left the room right about the same time her husband left. He was in the lounge and I chatted with him for a few moments. To get him out of ear shot, I asked if he'd like to walk with me to the other end of the hallway. I mentioned the new hospital and said "wouldn't it be cool if I could turn this old one into a place to help people get on their feet. It wouldn't be a homeless shelter or a free ride." He said "yeah, not like welfare. Each person would help and pay what they could." He and I talked as if we both were part of the same dream. We talked about what the rooms could be used for and the things people could be helped with. It was quite unusual and amazing at the same time.

A few days later, very early in the morning, I wrote 'I feel groggy from lack of sleep. Why do nurses feel the need to wake you from a sound rest by taking your vital signs? Linda loves watching TV but the noise grates against my nerves. My legs ache and I long for healing. I don't like being in the hospital but don't long to go back to life as it was. I don't know where to turn except to Jesus.'

Then I wrote this prayer "Jesus, You know all things pertaining to me and my life. You had it all planned before I was even born. You knit me together in my mother's womb and instilled every gift, talent, and trait - well all that I'd need for the lifetime I'd spend here in this natural world. You knew I'd be here, in this place. Nothing surprises You Lord! Whatever I do and wherever I go, I shall be led by Holy Spirit. My soul would like to have a plan in order to make decisions. My soul wants to understand the process and have clear direction. I suppose the battle of soul versus spirit still rages. I haven't a clue as to the purpose of these current life events. But Yahweh, You turn everything to the good. You are making me stronger and teaching me to trust. Even more, You're teaching me to be still and patient. I thought I had become lost (separated) in the wilderness, but I wasn't. Holy Spirit, You have always been with me. I am grateful for You. I realize how infinitely patient You are, but I only grasp a portion of that. I am amazed by You. Through all my grumbling, complaining, anger, and frustration, You still love and accept me. You waited for me to come back around."

It is trippy, and my mind struggled with understanding. Surely the tests and the proving ground served a valuable purpose. Healing will become such a part of me as will the humility and ability to give Yahweh all the glory and honor. He caused me (my spirit and soul) to rest. He allowed my body to rest too. I am fully dependent on Him. I needed to get alone with Him to rejuvenate, to heal, reconnect... What a journey this has been.

Looking back at the last several months, I see how I became lazy and lethargic. Attacks on my health plus Terry's apathetic spirit plus my lazy spirit equaled me feeling lost, disconnected, alone, and scared (in my mind anyway). In the middle of the battle, when I'd wanted to go to a church service, it seemed my body's symptoms would get worse. This seems to happen whenever the enemy is at work and the flesh is out of control. Yahweh allowed me to walk down that path. He helped me see how much I needed relationship with Him and how I needed guidance from Holy Spirit. He's made me look deeper/closer to every aspect or area of my life. I must decide what I value most. Yahweh must always come first. Since I'd been severely ill, I don't think I did that. Instead, I became self-absorbed, apathetic, and my full attention was garnered by other things. I utilized natural things (shows or movies) to distract my mind from the physical symptoms. Lord Jesus, I confess this to you and realize I missed the mark. It bothers me, really it angers me that I did this. I lost sight of Yahweh – the very One who created me and loves me unconditionally.

Finally, a new day dawned, and I prepared myself to leave the hospital. Before I left, Yahweh had another small task for me. Linda had to have a CT scan; her husband waited for her in the room with me. I chatted with him a bit then apologized for overhearing an earlier conversation between them (how couldn't you when you're in the same room). They'd discussed her psychiatric medications. I told him a little of my story and how I had received help and eventually weaned myself off them.

I didn't give advice or instruction for her to do the same. I simply encouraged them to research the medications. I also offered encouragement for Linda's journey.

It boggles my mind how Yahweh shifted people in order for me to end up in the same room with Linda. His perfect timing and divine intervention amaze me. Anyway, the time came for me to leave. It was Terry's birthday; to celebrate, we went out for lunch. We ordered and as we waited for our food, an older man walked by our table. He bent down, picked something up and said, "you dropped this" (I thought I heard him say quarter). He laid a nickel on the table. I stared at it for a few minutes and then looked at Terry. It was the oddest feeling. Terry smiled but didn't seem very excited and stated, "you know I don't get excited over much." I said, "look at what happened - - right here and now, that man, and the nickel; look at how it was orchestrated perfectly."

Terry asked, "but what does it mean?" I said, "I don't quite know. Think for a minute about Yahweh's perfect timing and how we were here at this precise moment, for that precise gentlemen, for that precise nickel to be placed on this precise table!" One thing for sure, Yahweh was letting me know that He is always with me!

REFLECTION

I feel lazy and out of sorts. I'm trying to take one day at a time, but it's not easy. Looking around, all I see is the chaos and mess of this unfinished house. You see, Terry's house is literally under construction. My spirit lives in a body with a soul, and just like the house, they too are under construction. I want and need a major change. I am concerned... are my spiritual senses dull? Lord help me! The more I am around Terry, the more I become like him. I wanted this to be the other way around. I want both of us to fully walk the spiritual lifestyle! However, I feel waylaid – disengaged from Yahweh's realm. It seems I lost the art of seeing/hearing what Daddy is saying or doing. That makes me sad. I don't like it! I am NOT where I want to be. I have struggled with dreaming or hoping. The battle to have faith and expectation frustrates me.

I feel like a lump on a log like I'm doing absolutely nothing except trying to stay alive. And Terry has sat beside me at times, not really knowing how to help me. I know I need to reengage with life (in both realms). I am weak and shaky (in the natural and the spiritual realm). I did NOT want this to happen! I don't understand how or why it did. I'm not sure how to escape, or even if I can. Does Daddy have me here for a reason? I want to run to Him and yell, "hold me, I need You! Help me out of this pit!! Show me the way!"

I stopped writing and drove to the river to write more and to spend time alone with Yahweh. It's quiet all around me. It's such a beautiful day! I stand at the river's edge and peer into the water. My reflection shows how weary I am. I think about the last several months. Night after night, day after day I suffered while I could barely cry out to Jesus for help. It seemed that I had walked through the valley of the shadow of death. I feel like I'm slowly waking from a dark and hurtful slumber. Abba (Daddy) is healing me as I remain tucked away (under His wing). Life (right here, right now) seems incredibly sweet. A cool breeze is blowing, the sun is shining, the birds are singing, and I find simple peace. A few boats float on the river, but no one is parked near me. Let me remain in Yahweh's Presence where nothing else matters. I look forward to taking walks with Jesus again. Oh to have Yahweh's full strength and grace back in my life. If I could, I would drink the sunshine.

I wish I could express the gravity of this recent challenge. It seemed I was in the darkest part of the night, then a light came on. The darkness hurried to hide, but a few shadows remained. Deep in my spirit, I know those shadows must go; they'll eventually fade away. Part of me is leery, concerned they will take over. However, deep down, I know I am protected in my Father's hands.

I look out across the water and a sailboat floats by. How effortlessly the wind moves it. A motorboat zooms past, trying to disrupt the serenity. The sailboat is unfazed. It is in no hurry as it soaks up the beauty and the sun. Its movements are gentle and easy going, like the way Holy Spirit moves us at times. I appreciate this moment even more <u>because</u> of the dark place I went through. Going through that seemed to calm or slow me down; it made me even more gentle. I am in peace and rest in my Father's Presence. Even through the worst time, He was with me.

He's increased my faith in Him.

I know now that Yahweh pulled me into a vacuum; it was like I was in a bubble, unaware of life going on around me. It was quiet and everyday events did not matter. I was tucked away in a secret place. While in that suffering, I fought simply to remain here in the natural realm. During the time of healing, I don't know all that Holy Spirit accomplished in me. Am I any different from the time before this? I know I am more dependent on the Lord. I am more mellow and reflective. I am more able to stay in the moment instead of looking at tomorrow's troubles. I trust Yahweh knows what is best for me. He knows what things must occur inside of me in order for me to accomplish what He's preordained for me. I hold nothing against Him, He will turn everything around. I release all reasoning, thus allowing Him to have His way and His will accomplished inside of me.

The spiritual life often clashes with the natural life. Yahweh has brought me to this place of complete reliance on Him; it required brokenness, humility, patience, commitment, trust, faith, grace, and love. I said before that I wanted to live in Yahweh's realm – to be fully immersed in this lifestyle. I want to be so full that I drip the oil of Him, let it ooze out of me – drip, drip, pour! What will it look like, feel like, or be like? I imagine the ability to taste colors and smell flavors. I long to consistently walk in His pure love, in full devotion and surrender to Jesus. I want to accomplish all of His works... to heal, raise the dead, and cast out demons. Oh my - to watch His loved ones realize they've been set free - in every way!

Awaken sleepy spirit I declare - - shake, shake, shake off the poisonous viper, that evil one of old. His venom is powerless and carries no sting. Shake off the old dust (religion) which can only trap, coat, and make one sneeze. My prayer is that all may be blessed to see they are bound no more. All are free to fly, dance, and sing praises to the King of kings, Lord Jesus! Everyone can return to the Father's heart and boldly step up to the Throne. In Him, we find incredible mercy, love, and grace. Freedom is not free; it was paid for by Christ and His great sacrifice!

As Galatians 2:20 states - Christ lives in me, it is His life and no longer mine. My life is so much richer from having gone through the valley of the shadow of death. While there, I did not fear evil for Jesus was with me, His rod and staff comforted me. Even though He's already showed me some things of the Kingdom, I remain hungry – oh my I'm hungry for more – oh more! I pray...

"Lord Jesus! I want to see You, hear You... I know You are with me even when my spiritual senses seem dull. The battle left me weak and weary; I carry the scars. I ask for grace and strength this day to do what You'd have me do. In Heaven, there's no illness, no mess, and no frustration. I call the gifts and fruits of Holy Spirit to pour forth. I release the wondering and worrying. I ask You to show me the next step and to wake up the provision inside of me. I admit, in my despair, I wanted free of this body - to come Home to You. It's not my will, but rather it is the Father's will to be done on earth as it is in Heaven!"

A DARK VALLEY

My first husband, Paul died from suicide on May 16, 2016. I met him when I was only 21 years old. That's more than half of my lifetime ago. He and I were like oil and water - as in we didn't mix very well. Still, the good Lord chose to put us together to bring Lindsey into the world. Upon hearing of his death, my mind reviewed his and my history.

Paul was nine years older than me. He had been in the Marines and had a lifetime of experiences before I even met him. It wasn't long after we met that he wanted to marry. Our daughter, Lindsey, was born two days before our one-year anniversary. She was six weeks early, and Paul was very protective. He even made everyone wash their hands before they could hold her. Our marriage only lasted five years. I'm amazed it lasted that long <u>because</u> we were opposites.

Back then the years seemed to crawl along but looking back I realize they, in fact, flew by. Paul hadn't made that passage of time easy. And there were moments (back then) that I had an intense dislike (even hatred) of the man. We had many arguments and clashes. Once Lindsey turned 18, it was a relief that I no longer had to battle with him. Then one day, a life altering event took place.

On Father's Day of 2010, Paul and his girlfriend were in a tragic accident. A drunk motorcyclist hit Paul's motorcycle at a speed more than 100 mph. Paul's girlfriend was thrown into oncoming traffic, hit, and killed. Paul was in grave danger of losing his life as well. Lindsey called to tell me the news and asked me to drive her and her husband, Nick, to the New Jersey hospital. I didn't hesitate. I didn't think of the past or wrongs done. I just drove (probably a little too fast). After a few weeks, Paul was moved to a hospital in Pennsylvania, closer to home. He spent around forty days in the hospital. I visited him often. I took him some of his belongings and was simply there for him. When he left the hospital, he was taken to his brother's home. I continued to visit with him. I helped him process the loss of his loved one.

Somewhere along the way I had completely forgiven and let go of the past. He and I became friends. The old junk was completely gone and healed. This amazes me, and I can only point to Yahweh's grace as the reason this occurred. I am grateful that Paul and I made peace. I'm grateful I was able to help him and show him Christ's love.

Paul was buried on May 22nd with military honors. Lindsey was pregnant with her third child. I was physically weak (still healing from diverticulitis). But my thoughts weren't on my condition. I was glad I could stand beside her that day. It was difficult. The words spoken, the honor given, the gun salute, the folded flag - all caused tears and deep breaths.

Death is a wake-up call to those still living; it makes you appreciate life. Paul's death made me take a closer look at my life. I felt as though I had been living in a rut. But, I wanted to live life more fully and have more experiences. I sense a shaking starting. It's like I'm standing on uneven ground that is rumbling awake. Certain experiences have shown up in dreams, although my mind can't recall the exact scenes. An unsettled feeling resides deep in my chest. Shake, shake, shake; change is coming.

Still, this seemingly stagnant existence brings a prevailing sadness over me. It covers me like an unwanted woolly blanket worn in the heat of the summer. I can't seem to shake it off. It clings to me and anxiety grips my gut. What is going on?!

Finally, I relax and decide not to fight with it. I can't discern what is happening. My prayers are that the dream Yahweh has for me will be fulfilled swiftly. It's 'funny' that I've been reading Job. In chapter thirty-eight, Yahweh asks, "who are you?" He laid the foundations of the earth. He commands the sea and sets its limits. He orchestrates the sun, moon, and stars. He can access the deepest parts of the sea. Who do we think we are to question Him? I am but a vapor; here today and gone tomorrow.

Yahweh works on the things of this world, He similarly does internal work in each of us. He's completed work inside of me that I wasn't even aware needed to be done. It is a dark sea at times, this place He has me. I close my eyes and swim looking for Him. He is here. That sea of love becomes my breath, my blood, my sweat, my tears... It is like the birthing experience - at the height of labor when the mother just wants the process over with. It's the deep groaning and striving to produce new life. Yet, throughout that process, there are moments to rest. Each and every moment, every single breath, push, rest, and moan is necessary and needed. Whether you're talking about the actual birthing process or a spiritual birthing, the process slowly changes, molds, and prepares you. I am not sure which is harder - the natural or the spiritual. I never liked the raw moments, where I could barely move! These seemed to be the worst, yet the best (because they are essential to my growth).

In this spiritual process, I don't even know exactly what is being birthed. Maybe it will be a new ME. What will I look like?

Hopefully, I'll end up looking like Jesus.

When we walk through a dark valley, the journey can be nearly too much to absorb or bear. What have I learned thus far? What tests have I processed? I know and believe that I am seated with Christ in Heavenly places. He has given me a purpose and destiny. He has appointed me for such a time as this and has given me a sphere of influence. In other words, I can influence those around me. I've learned before that what the Lord takes us through, He gives us victory in - and not only for ourselves but for others.

Several days after Paul's funeral, pain showed up in my left side again. I didn't know what was going on; I worried diverticulitis was back. A few nights after that, Terry rolled over and his foot touched me. I was having trouble 'coming to' and awoke saying "help me!" It wasn't really fear I experienced; it was as if my spirit was on a 'walk about' and the body was trying to wake up without me. It seemed my spirit had a hard time reentering this hurting body. Where does my spirit go when I dream? Do I walk through the valley or am I on the mountain top? I want to continue in the Heavenly places, walking with Jesus. Even as I write this, it sounds strange. Who thinks like this?

Several weeks after Paul's funeral, Lindsey, Terry, and I began the process of clearing her dad's trailer out. I wondered about his last years living alone in an unfinished trailer. He had been working on it, but his accident (in 2010) derailed his plans. He must have been frustrated looking at his home day after day while knowing he was unable to complete what he'd started. After all, he had been a Marine and was used to having things a certain way. What were his last moments like in that place? While no other human was there, I'm sure the Lord didn't let Paul die alone. Yahweh is always with us, and I believe He made Himself known to Paul in his last moments on earth.

What will my last moments in this world be like? I pray to have already accomplished the plans and purpose the Lord sent me to do. When I take the last gasp of earthly air and breathe in Heaven's air, will I see my life flash before my eyes? Will the images be of the natural world? Maybe they'll contain spiritual realm pictures. Maybe I'll see both. I don't want to wait till it's too late. I don't want any regrets.

After the 1st clean out day was done, and I had about worn myself out, I went home to rest. I watched the movie "War Room" again. It reminded me of the authority I carry. Whenever I fight with my frail body, I tend to forget who I am. I had let down my guard and this watch-woman dozed on the wall. "Lord, forgive me, I forgot for a moment Who You are." I thought for a second that the enemy won a skirmish. Nope - Jesus already had won the war.

When I laid in my sick bed, I worried I'd let my spirit slumber while my body rested and healed. But Holy Spirit, never stopped working - I can't even wrap my mind around all He did while I was in that dark valley. I don't have to feel condemned because He does not condemn me.

I trust that every part of me was in Daddy's capable hands. I trust that Holy Spirit did such a deep internal work inside of me - to mold me into the warrior Yahweh designed me to be. I refuse to accept the lies, shame or blame the enemy tries to heap onto my head. I praise Jesus for awakening me and I look forward (not in reverse).

"I pray for Lindsey in this time of grief and great need. I ask You, Lord, to strengthen her; give her grace and let her see You at work. I pray health and healing for her little ones. Encourage their little hearts. Let Lindsey teach them Your ways. I pray for Angelica, Lord, I know that she is highly favored by You. Turn her eyes always back to You. Let her see You! I pray for her little ones, let them be taught of You Lord. I pray for my husband Terry, continue to work in him. Help him to walk this faith journey and help him to see You. Thank you for blessing the work of his hands and spilling an abundance of Your provision into him. Daddy, I adore You. You are worthy and deserving of all praise, honor, and glory. I am amazed by You. Thank You, Daddy - for You. Help me to consistently be aware of You, teach me to pray the Words of Your heart. Give me Your battle cry. As I walk forth, let me be aware of the armor I carry and the tools at my disposal. You are a good Father. I turn away from doubt and unbelief. I know and believe that absolutely nothing can separate me from Your great love."

DIVING DEEPER

Recently Terry, Cheryl (my sister), Larry (her husband), and I visited Crystal Cave in Kutztown PA. While we were deep in the depths of that dark cave, the guide pointed out that the rock just above us had shifted (fallen somewhat) over 1,000 years ago due to an earthquake. How do they know that? It's not like they had an eyewitness. Anyway, further down the cave path, we all got a different view of that rock. It was <u>huge</u>, possibly the size of a large house. Even further down the path, after some instructions, the guide turned out the lights. I couldn't see Terry's face, which was right in front of me. I realized two important facts. 1) We see things from our perspective, but Yahweh's perspective is much larger. Certainly, He knows much more than we do. 2) There are none so blind as those who will not see. I'm not sure how this all connects yet - but I do know that Holy Spirit is in the midst of it all.

Today is a new day. I take a deep breath soaking in the quiet of the morning. I ponder how hectic my life has been, with one thing happening after another. It's like being in an angry ocean, being tossed to and fro and finally hitting the rocks on the shore, unsure if I'll survive or go under and at times wishing for the latter. I much prefer the stillness, the silence - where I am able to center my thoughts on Jesus. I long to walk and talk with Him, to allow His quiet peace to settle upon me. Feeling full of Holy Spirit, it seems I can breathe again. His grace, comfort, and peace are my blood. How I long to remain in Yahweh's Presence - alone and free from the world's troubles. Instead, I allow myself to be drawn back into the natural reality of my circumstances. It's very unsettling and I find it difficult to be content there. Mostly, it seems life has just happened to me. Don't I have any say or control? For too many years I did not know what the vision of my life could be. I just knew wherever I landed, it seemed I could say "this isn't it." Sigh, I know I can't look to circumstances to define or please me. I can't look to others to fulfill this great need inside of me. I need the searchlight of Holy Spirit to illuminate the deep recesses of me. What needs done? What do I really want? All I can answer is that I don't want what I currently have. It makes me feel disappointed, sad, lost, and alone. If one doesn't know what one wants or where one wants to go - how can you begin going?

I still imagine Rae of Hope (explained in my last book). At times I have questioned, doubted, and even surrendered it. Then I would pick it back up, dream, envision, hope, and pray some more. I continue to stand in agreement with Yahweh about His dream for me. Yet, I feel stuck in an unfinished house, not knowing which way to go. What action(s) can I take? Am I free to take risks? I have full faith that Yahweh can do all He has said He will do. I'm reminded of Gideon. Yahweh saw him as a mighty warrior, but Gideon saw himself as weak. Is this the same for me?

I've wasted too many days going around and around trying to find a viable solution to my living situation. I've been frustrated, sick, and tired of it all. It seems I am diving deeper and deeper into muddy waters and I don't like it. What risks can I take? Where will I go and what will I do? These feelings have caused several conflicts between Terry and me. I find that my sleep is troubled because my mind is not at rest - it consistently tries to work out a solution. Whenever I engage Terry, it becomes a battle of misunderstanding; and miscommunication rules the day. My physical body feels the full impact of stress and strain. After each skirmish, I walk away hurt and frustrated. The key is to go back again into the fray after emotions have departed. I recognize that when old baggage is buried, often it is not dead. Somehow, like Lazarus, the baggage comes to life or will surface again until it is dealt with completely.   Many times, I have asked Holy Spirit to deal with the wound, trauma, or whatever is hidden inside of me. Whenever an old wound is left buried, it will fester like a deep infection in the root of a tooth. It's unbearable when it awakes or reaches a tipping point.

Why does the Lord utilize conflict in relationships to deal with old baggage? Even after the dust settles for a little while, suddenly, another bag (suitcase) is brought up out of the depths. A simple request for a kiss from Terry at an inopportune moment caused a minor conflict between us. Holy Spirit made me look at the whole picture and ask hard questions once again. I really don't like this process. Terry and I talked about the whole situation, but I really didn't know what was in that particular suitcase.

What is this issue or deep-rooted problem? I asked the Lord to dive deeper and reveal what is hidden from my view. His answer was "you have often felt unloved or unlovable." He showed me that I carried a humongous burden of conditional love which made me feel unworthy and hopeless. I could see no way to be all that someone else wanted me to be.

When you can't quite measure up, it leaves you with such an awful feeling. It makes you enter a place of striving, people pleasing, and perfectionism - all of which are futile.   No amount of effort can change another's perception. If we could, then we'd be 'earning' their love.

When someone has not experienced (or realized they experienced) unconditional love, they can't believe it even exists. It is such a foreign concept to them. In that state, anyone would have trouble believing or trusting Yahweh's Agape love. It is hard to open oneself up to the concept that they don't have to be a certain way or do certain things to have Yahweh's love. Many aren't willing to take the risk of being that vulnerable. For most, it's hard to imagine that truly all things are permissible, yet not all things are beneficial - 1 Corinthians 10:23. We cannot mess up enough to lose Yahweh's love for us.

The process of fully realizing and experiencing Yahweh's love has just begun for me. I may have known it in my mind, but the knowing must dive deeper into my heart. I mustn't look to Terry or anyone else for approval or acceptance. My value doesn't come from them. I am worthy because Yahweh has made me worthy. I need not remain in the hopeless cave or be alone in the dark. Hope is being confident that Yahweh will fulfill His promises. While people may let us down, Yahweh is forever faithful. I now have the power to understand how wide, how long, how high, and how deep Yahweh's love is - Ephesians 3:18.

YAHWEH'S GIFTS

Joy and I went to the Stirring conference at Global Awakening. On the way there we agreed that we'd like to sit somewhere different from our usual seats. As we stood in line, I noticed a small group of women at the front of the line. As they were talking, another woman who started out behind us, slowly worked her way to the others and joined in their conversation. Soon, the doors opened, and everyone headed in. Joy and I purposefully walked up a row and chose seats different from where we had ever sat. These seats just so happened to be the same ones that woman (who'd gotten herself in front of the line) wanted. She was quite determined and put her belongings on the 3rd seat in. Well at first, I figured she was giving up the seats (the two Joy and I wanted). I sat down, and she said she wanted to sit on the end, but I'd already claimed the 1st two seats. To be polite, I stood up to let her get to the 3rd seat. She literally pushed me out of the way to take over all three seats. Joy was belly laughing! I could hardly believe what happened. We walked away and went back to the front, in the area where we normally sit. Joy sat down but then we shifted over just a few seats.

Before the service started, I spoke aloud saying something like "Lord I refuse to pick up an offense over what that lady did. So, I give it all to You Yahweh." Soon the worship team started playing so we stood to join in. At one point during the worship service, I looked for Joy, but she had disappeared. It was at that exact moment I smelled the scent of Frankincense. It was as if it was pouring down from the ceiling on top of me. I took great big breaths of it and looked around to see if anyone else smelled it. Everyone around me seemed oblivious to it. I was smiling, full of joy; and one lady told me that I looked like an angel. Finally, I noticed Joy as she sat in her chair. She looked amazed and was crying happy tears. She told me why she'd disappeared - a lady approached her and said, "I have something for you, come outside with me." Joy hesitated but went. The lady gave her a flash drive with four of Randy Clark's books on it and a CD teaching set on healing! It wasn't long ago that Brad, Joy's husband, had been diagnosed with stage four colon cancer. These gifts deeply encouraged Joy. We both were astonished at Yahweh's timing, love, and sense of humor.

When the worship music ended, I asked Joy "who gave you these things?" She looked around and the lady was sitting right next to me! Another lady (sitting close to us) told me that she'd noticed my tattoo and thought it was of Michael the archangel (which it is). She then said when I was dancing, a blue light (representing him) was around me. She stated that he's been my protector and around me my whole life. I find that interesting, but I know that Michael (the archangel) is the protector of Israel. Angels are not omnipresent, but maybe they can move quickly through the atmosphere.

Later, in the conference, Joy and I sat next to another lady. This lady and I chatted for a bit. She revealed something odd. She said many people have been offended by her. I tried to encourage her, but she seemed determined to remain in that mindset. Later, she proved what she'd meant. Somehow the seating got a little mixed up and she was left without her seat. She was struggling to figure out who's stuff she could move. She picked my things. I politely said: "honey, that's mine." I truly was willing to take my things and sit on the floor. She said, "Be quiet, I am trying to think!" She got aggravated and moved to another area.

The next day, Joy and I reserved our seats early then went outside. When we came back in, a different lady was sitting next to the seats we'd reserved. Just as I walked in, she was moving our things. I don't know why, but I said to her "those are our things." She said, "I didn't move them." I said, "I just saw you move them." She was flustered; I was amused. It took a few moments to realize that offense wanted to take over. She and I got past the awkwardness and could make light of the whole situation.

It is funny how people will become territorial over their seats. You'd almost expect that in a secular setting, but to see it in a Christian conference?! Why are believers acting the same or doing the same things as non-believers? Shouldn't we stand out - in a good way? Shouldn't we willing give up our seat for another?

Looking back at that conference, one of the best gifts Yahweh gave me was the ability to see 'offense' in action. I really didn't feel offended, upset, or angry at any of the people. I even laughed over the silliness of it all. In the future, I hope I do not pick up any offense. I can't give offense if it's not in me <u>to</u> give away. I hope to only give Holy Spirit's fruit to others.

SECRET OF CONTENTMENT

Where does time go? Does it actually go anywhere? Upon finding oneself in an uncomfortable place, how do you become content? I have been going around this same mountain for way too long. It's the giant mountain of stagnation or lethargy. It seems I've just been wasting time. I don't think I'm accomplishing anything important. It doesn't seem like I am growing in my faith, going anywhere, or that I am utilizing my spiritual gifts. I am not content in this unmoving pool. I would rather be riding the white-water rapids! I never dreamed of being in such a still place -how did I end up here!? Certainly, no one made me make the choices that landed me here. And while many hard things have happened to me, I refuse to play the victim.

Yet, I can't help but feel foolish as though I have been duped. You see, I agreed to marry Terry because I believed we'd set out on a unique spiritual journey together. The vows we made to each other were spiritual in nature. We promised we'd seek Yahweh and discover the adventures He has for us. Unfortunately, this has not happened. I tried to demonstrate this incredible walk of faith. But Terry is caught in the natural day-to-day rut of life. Not only am I frustrated, I am sad for him. He doesn't realize what he's missing. I was hoping he'd want to change. But instead of him changing, I have become more like him. I find myself floating in the lazy river of life.

Okay, now that I acknowledge the facts, what new choices must I make? I could stay in this stagnated existence or I could move forward. I'm not sure Terry and I should live separately for a time. And I don't know if living apart would help either of us in our individual faith journey. Obviously, Terry's not done much up to this point. I seriously doubt he will make an effort no matter what our living arrangement is.

I've been told that if Terry and I separate AND we don't have purposeful and meaningful interaction during the time apart, we'd be living in a state of divorce. Either option could give the enemy an opportunity to steal and destroy. I don't know if we should remain married and work on our relationship. Or should we divorce and move on. This is not a simple choice.

I don't see how I can make such a difficult decision. It's just too hard! Yet, I can't seem to be content with the way things are. I don't want to stay in the stagnant pool or ride in the lazy river out of fear of what's outside of those places. But, for real, what is there to fear? Maybe I need to face the imaginary fears of failure, being alone, financial uncertainty or ending up in worse circumstances. I do not want fear to stop me! I want to trust Yahweh in each moment as it comes. I can't hide my head in the sand, but I don't want to land in a dark place. And I really do not want to abort Yahweh's process. What <u>can</u> I do…

Okay, let me review an option. Maybe I can live in my travel trailer at a campground. A quick search on the internet revealed a few possible campsites. Thinking about it freaks me out a little. What a big step this would be. I have no idea what it would be like. All I know for certain is I am no longer content with status quo. I am weary of the 'just enough' day-to-day life. I need to become all Yahweh has designed me to be. Perhaps I can take a leap of faith, just jump into a new future with both feet. On one hand, I am excited about the possibilities. On the other hand, I am angry that I am in such a difficult decision-making process. I have no clue what I should do.

Stress from this internal struggle weighs heavy on me. This causes my entire body to ache, and I am left feeling washed out. I push myself to envision living alone in a campground. I don't know if it would be as I imagine. I don't know if I would be content living that way. I suppose I should talk to Terry about these things. That's hard for me to do as I'm tired of his empty promises. His inaction to fix up his house or make any other move forward shows his lethargy in the spirit as well. Once again, I see how the natural mirrors the spiritual realm.

I pray, "search my heart, Holy Spirit. I need Your wisdom and guidance. I don't doubt You or what YOU can do. It doesn't look like Terry's utilized the faith You instilled in him."

I'm reminded of the Israelites journey in the wilderness. That journey should have lasted eleven days. But, the journey, in fact, took forty years. They longed for the leeks, cucumbers, and garlic of Egypt. They even longed for their old captivity. When it was time to leave the wilderness and go into the promised land, they were afraid of the giants that lived there. I don't want to go backwards (into my old captivity). And I don't want to get stuck in the wilderness because I'm afraid of what's in the land ahead.

Finally, I gave in and talked to Terry. I told him about this battle and how it seems he and I keep going back to the same mountain. I reminded him I never wanted to live in his house and I don't want to walk down the path he has chosen. I believe he is content living his life the way he has been living. He told me he doesn't want to lose me. But those words seem empty. He's made very little effort to help me feel content, safe, or secure. When I said I wanted to move the travel trailer to a local campground, he only said: "if that's what you want." Cut and dry, no discussion; nor did he present other possibilities. It's not simple and never has been. I could only ask myself "what is going on here?" The plot thickens...

After I talked with Terry, I went to a friends' house for a worship and teaching service. It was very hot, and I passed out. A nurse, who was there, thought I had a seizure. I disagreed. I can't help but wonder where I went when I passed out. And what happened while I was there? This event made no sense and my wondering produced no solutions.

When I got home and told Terry, he claimed he realized he'd needed a wake-up call. Then why the heck was I the one to pass out? I ended up calling my Doctor even though I really didn't want to. Of course, he insisted on an EEG being done. The results showed some abnormality. A few days later, I received a letter from the Department of Motor Vehicles; I had to surrender my driver's license!

Why didn't I throw a fit? Well... first off, what would be the point. Secondly, I had learned a lesson from Joy not long ago. She had wanted to run away from home, but her car broke down. At that time, I was reading in Exodus how the Lord took the Pharaoh's chariots wheels. Not much longer after her car broke down, her husband was diagnosed with cancer. Of course, Yahweh does not cause evil things to happen. Instead, He always turns the bad to good. The loss of Joy's wheels allowed her to help Brad during his cancer treatments.

So… why did I lose my 'wheels?' I thought I had built a pretty strong case for leaving; after all Terry hadn't done what he said he would. It really wasn't fair that I was the one this happened to. Not only was I stuck in Terry's house, I was dependent on him (and others) to get me to appointments, the store, and so on. Oh brother, talk about the opposite of what I wanted!!!

Despite everything, <u>somehow,</u> I simply accepted the fact I wasn't allowed to drive. This was my only option. Still, many questions swirled around in my mind. My main question was "why?" Perhaps I was wrong in wanting to leave. The struggle to stay put and be content has been on-going. I don't know if I can accept that THIS is where Yahweh might want me to be. I have been saying I don't want to focus on the natural. I need help to focus my eyes on Daddy's face and see what He's doing. It may be that my husband, our relationship, this house, these lessons, and so on relate to my purpose for being on this earth at this time.

If our words have creative power - and I believe they do - what should I say or do. Look at Luke 9:23 - if we are to follow Jesus, we must not go our own way, but instead take up our cross daily. The cross was Jesus' purpose (the reason He came to earth as a man). We're not called to be crucified. The cross we carry is Yahweh's purpose for us. Will I take up my cross and follow Jesus (walk as He did and finish my race)? I suppose I still have much to learn. Holy Spirit continued to teach and 'show off'…

Not long after I turned my license in, Terry and I headed out to attend a small church service. As he drove, he talked about Ellis Island and a little about politics. During the sermon, the Pastor mentioned the Statue of Liberty, the welcoming of those weary souls, and how Jesus welcomes us all. He reminded us to be careful of our thoughts as they can turn into actions when we speak them.

Later, I found myself asking the same question. What is the secret of contentment? The Israelites weren't content in Egypt, and they weren't content in the wilderness. Clearly, I ended up stuck in my own wilderness for any number of reasons that only the Lord must know. I thought I had a way out of the mess until the fainting episode. Instead, I was forced to be still in the secret place of Yahweh's Presence.

Connections are signs used to direct our attention back to Yahweh. We can take notice of what He is doing. Circumstances are used to teach us to trust Jesus - He already has provided all we need. I don't want to wander around forty years like the Israelites. Jesus was in the wilderness only 40 days. Before He entered the wilderness, the Father clearly established Jesus' identity - Matthew 3:17, Mark 1:11, Luke 3:22. While Jesus was in the wilderness, He had no complaints. He didn't miss the mark (sin) despite being tempted by the devil. How was He content in that place?

Paul (of the Bible) learned to be content no matter what circumstances he found himself in. He learned the **secret** of being content in any situation. What's the secret? We can do all things (including being content) through Christ who strengthens us. - Philippians 4:11-13. We aren't doing this alone. We can enter any wilderness (situation) fully established in our identity in Christ. To be content means "sufficient for one's self, strong enough or possessing enough to need no aid or support; independent of external circumstances, contented with one's means." [1]

I understand that my circumstances, living arrangements, other people, etcetera are not what will cause me to be content. I should not be rattled by anything to the point of becoming discontent. Contentment is built deep inside of us; it's built on a foundation of love and trust in and for Yahweh. No matter where I go or what I must walk through, I can find contentment in the fact that I have the help of Jesus who strengthens me. Honestly, this concerns me because I don't know what trials, tests, or tribulations await me in the future. All I can do is take the next step and ask Holy Spirit to help me be content.

NOTE

[1] G842 - autarkēs - Strong's Greek Lexicon (KJV). Retrieved from https://www.blueletterbible.org//lang/Lexicon/Lexicon.cfm?Strongs=G842&t=KJV

SAMSON

Terry and I along with Cheryl (my sister) and her husband Larry went to see Samson at the Sight and Sound Theater in Lancaster PA. We had been looking forward to going since we'd first ordered the tickets. We arrived early, so we meandered around just checking out the surroundings. Finally, it was time to be seated. Our seats were up high in the balcony section; Cheryl and I had to be careful because looking down made both of us feel dizzy. It's funny how we thought the show would last a long time, but before we knew it, it was over. Every actor and actress, and every person behind the scenes completed their jobs to perfection. What an amazing show! I highly recommend this Theater!

Anyway… It's odd how the show "Samson" was timely in my present moment of trials. <u>Of course</u>, the Lord would find things to teach me. Hidden within Samson's story, I am certain some lessons will apply to my story. I thought I knew most of Samson's story. I'd heard of his incredible strength and how he saved the day at the end of his life. Certainly, there's always more to learn. So, I opened my Bible to the story of Samson in the book of Judges.

Samson's parents were righteous; still, his mother had been barren until an angel of the Lord told her she'd become pregnant and have a son. Can you even imagine this scene? My mother was far from being barre; she had eight children! I can only imagine her response if she'd been told as a young teen that she'd end up with eight children. It makes me giggle to think of it. My mother was quite the character. I can see her giving an angel a 'piece of her mind.'

As Samson grew up, the Lord blessed him and "stirred" inside Samson. This is one of the things that make you question - what in the world does that mean? I just had to look it up. Stirred, in the original language, means "to thrush, impel, push, beat persistently, agitate, move or trouble" [1]. Well, that is weird! Does the Lord actually do things like this? Yep of course He does.

Samson obviously knew the Lord and knew what he should do or not do. I'm certain his parents taught him well. However, Samson chose to step outside of his faith and marry a Philistine woman. Maybe you've wondered, why he was willing to defy Yahweh's will. Why do we step outside of Yahweh's perfect will for our lives? Too many times I have gone my own way and ended up in quite the debacle. Looking closer at Samson's life, I found another situation he'd gotten himself into...

Samson was upset because when he was away from his wife, she'd been given to another man. Seriously, things like that happened and the stories are in the Bible! Samson was upset by the loss of his wife, so he caught 300 foxes, tied their tails together (in pairs) and fastened torches to their tails. Then he set them loose. The fire burned down the Philistine's grain fields and destroyed their vineyards and olive groves. The fire in the foxes' tails destroyed the Philistines livelihood. I try to imagine the scene; my first thought was 'those poor foxes.' I know, silly me. Then I thought of Samson. He must have been very angry to do such a deed. Then I thought of the Philistines. They probably were devastated as the damage must have been astronomical. I wonder how long and how far the fire burned. I wonder how much damage it caused. Why didn't the Philistines turn to the Lord for help? Samson meant this to be an act of revenge. The Lord allowed these things to happen to the Philistines (the enemy). Wrapping my mind around this fact is hard. Clearly, I don't have the full picture.

When I look back at my mistakes, was the Lord there, working against the enemy? I've not thought of this before. I hadn't seen the possibility that Yahweh's could have used my fumbles to destroy the enemy's camp. I imagine there are hundreds of times Yahweh intervened and helped me in my life. Wow, to think He would use my mistakes to take out the enemy is a whole new idea to me.

As I read, I noticed something about Samson's story that I'd not seen before. Samson slept with a prostitute - clearly, that wasn't Yahweh's plan! (See Judges 16:1.) This action shows Samson stepped even further outside of Yahweh's will. The Lord is very patient with all of us. No matter what we do, we can't lose His love.

Then Samson fell in love with Delilah. I wonder if he really knew what love was. Delilah clearly was not the best choice he could have made. She was promised 1,100 pieces of silver (from every one of the Philistine leaders) to discover the secret of Samson's strength. It took her four times to discover the secret. Samson certainly wasn't an ignorant man. Why did he keep playing games with Delilah? Why didn't he just get away from her? Instead, he stayed in the enemy's camp and got his head shaved. He KNEW if his head were shaved he'd lose his strength - Judges 16:17. But when the Philistines came in to capture him (on their fourth try), he didn't realize that the Lord had departed from him. Seriously?

In Deuteronomy 31:8, we learn that the Lord will not leave or forsake us. Is there a conflict here? Well, Yahweh made it clear what his guidelines were for the Israelites (see Deuteronomy 28). He gave them a choice - they could choose life and blessings OR death and curses. He wanted them to choose life. There are consequences for doing what is wrong, and there are rewards for doing what is right. There is a principle of reaping what one sows (the world calls this karma). We don't have to worry about following the religious laws per se. Instead, we can have a close and personal relationship with our Creator!

As I think about the hair chopping scenario, I wonder - did Samson really think the strength came from his hair. Didn't he realize the strength actually came from Yahweh? What do we put our belief or hope in? Are we like the little elephant in the movie "Dumbo", thinking some 'thing' gives us special abilities? That little elephant believed a feather helped him to fly. Don't we know that all our talent, ability, strength, gifts, and fruit come from Yahweh?! Amazingly, because of Jesus' sacrifice, no matter how many times we fall, Yahweh's grace is sufficient to pick us back up.

At the very end of his story - Judges 16:30, Samson asked the Lord to let him die with the Philistines. Why did he pray this? Why did Yahweh honor his prayer? I'm not sure I can discern the answers to these questions.

I must look at why I pray the things I do; where is my heart in those prayers. Do I ask for things I shouldn't - or for things outside of Yahweh's perfect will? Does Yahweh answer my prayers; yes, I believe He does. His answer may not be the one I want to hear. His answer is certainly above all I could fully discern. His ways are not my ways.

I may stumble and fall. I may soar like the eagle. I may sit beside still waters. At times I don't know what to expect and I suppose that is the secret of the walk of faith. No matter what I experience and no matter what my circumstances, I can relax knowing I'm tucked under Yahweh's protective wing. I can't predict the future, and most times I can't discern the past. But I do know that Yahweh is working His purpose out for me in this life. I long for more; a deeper relationship with Him. If he were to "stir" me like He did Samson, what would that be like. Maybe I have already been stirred. I trust Him, so I'm willing to move forward.

I took a break from writing this story and downloaded a new book. I only read the first paragraph of the Prologue and I am undone. I am laughing and crying all at the same time. Wouldn't you know Yahweh had a message for me in those words. I discovered (again) that Yahweh <u>wants</u> to heal the wounds of my heart (soul). As I am healed, any obstacle will be removed from my soul which caused me to feel blocked from Yahweh, and I will begin to experience a deeper relationship with Him. As this occurs, I'll be able to be more connected to Terry and others. I don't expect it to be an easy process as I need to abandon walls, barriers, locks, fear, and so on. It's like I am jumping off the cliff into thin air with Yahweh as my parachute. It's like being in a smoke-filled room with fire all around me with Holy Spirit as my air and Jesus as my Rescuer.

I'm not sure how to navigate the days ahead. So, like a young girl, I run to Abba (Daddy); my hair a mess, arms swinging every which way, legs gangly, and knees knocking. I run to Him unashamed as I abandon the invisible chains. I release all my cares, every single worry, all the control, and discontent. I just breathe it all out and let it all go. Now, I sense His Presence, I breathe Him in. He is the air I breathe. His peace settles over me and in every part of me. His kindness is incredible. I feel welcomed in His embrace.

NOTE

[1] H6470 - pa`am - Strong's Hebrew Lexicon (KJV). Retrieved from https://www.blueletterbible.org//lang/Lexicon/Lexicon.cfm?Strongs=H6470&t=KJV

COVERING

This past Sunday, there were two options of where to attend church services. Terry didn't feel comfortable with the one; I decided not to fight against him. It is an odd feeling to let my husband choose where we should go. It was odd that I felt no need to do my own thing. When we arrived at the service, the Pastor told me if I get a word or see something from the Lord, I was free to speak. Wow, that hasn't happened before. Was there a connection? Well, by following Terry's lead (and not arguing), then having the Pastor's permission, I was again able to 'see.'

During worship, I pictured a shiny gold crown; then it became the top of a carousel of sorts. But it didn't have the typical animals and seats. Instead, depicted were unique gifts from Yahweh. I wanted to share what I'd seen, but I was nervous to share in front of the group. Terry encouraged me and even walked part of the way up with me. The entire first service was simply worship music, and it was great!

During the second worship service, I saw another picture and 'heard' a few words from the Lord. I didn't step up to share because it felt 'showy.' Instead, I prayed a basic prayer "Lord, if you want me to share this, You'll have to make an opportunity."

After the second service, the Pastor held baptism services. As each one was baptized, they were prayed for and encouraging (prophetic) words were spoken over them. I was hungry and tired, but Terry wanted to stay. Rebecca entered the baptism pool and a few people said the Lord was giving her a new name or something new. After a few moments, the Pastor leaned over, looked at me, and motioned for me to come up. Immediately, I knew what I'd seen and heard during the 2nd worship service was for Rebecca. I said to her "the world says you can't remove the spots from a leopard, but Jesus already has. And a tiger has stripes, but Jesus took the stripes for us. He has created a new you." After the baptism service, Terry and I ate lunch with the group. It was very nice to eat, talk, and just fellowship with them.

Later that day, Terry pointed out that the whole day began with my letting him decide where we'd attend services. He realized that in the past, I probably would have argued my case for the other church. This was huge as I tend to be fairly independent.

I realize that my trusting decision led to Terry and me going to the service, to the Pastor giving me permission to speak, to my giving encouraging words for the group and for Rebecca. I realize that the Lord has made changes in Terry, me, and our marriage. He and I are being molded into what Yahweh designed us to be. As each of us is prepared and proven, we will become powerful weapons in Yahweh's Kingdom. These weapons are ones of grace, love, and mercy with the full character and integrity of Jesus. These weapons will help us to win back His people and to help them realize how very active Holy Spirit is.

I've held the dream of "Rae of Hope" close to my heart. While I have always been willing to share this dream with others, somehow, I'd not seen anyone but me at the helm. I have learned I will not be alone in that mission field. My loved ones and family of believers all could play a part and share in the gifts, promises, and purpose of Rae of Hope. In the past, I worried about someone (specifically a man) taking the promise (and more) from me. I am beginning to understand that whatever Yahweh has for me cannot be taken away. I also realize that the dream is Yahweh's – designed and created by Him. The way I have imagined it may not be the way it will unfold. I have to let the vision pour out of me however Yahweh wishes for it to pour out.

It's now late in the evening. As the sun goes down, quiet comes over the land. For reasons only He knows, Holy Spirit has brought "Jane" to my mind and heart. I ask Him "Lord, what do you want to show me." Jane has many broken places inside of her. As a result, she's dealt with obsessive compulsive thoughts for many years. Two of her problems may seem teeny tiny in the natural, yet they are huge mountains to her. These have ruled her for over 10 years and fear has reigned strong in her life.

I picture Jane as though she's fallen from a boat into a stormy sea. She's slowly drowning as she flails about. She cannot swim and desperately searches for someone to jump in to rescue her out of her obsession. However, she'd drag under anyone who would get close to her. Someone from the boat must throw her a life preserver - namely, Jesus as only He can keep her afloat. He is our life Savior and Preserver. Plus, He can walk on water!!

I have thrown the Life Preserver to her time and time again. I have tried to help her see Who Yahweh is and who He has created her to be. Certainly, I am not who she needs. She has gained a short victory here or there, but it seems she always returns to the sea. I have done all I know to do - point her to Jesus. Yes, often we need a voice to encourage us and Yahweh has given us one another. We can speak what we hear the Father says and do what He is doing. But we cannot do for someone else what is necessary for them to do. We cannot make someone believe what they refuse to believe. It's frustrating because I can clearly see in the spirit who Yahweh created Jane to be. I have shared that information with her. It doesn't seem to change her or her situation.

If you believe less of yourself than what Yahweh says about you, I greatly encourage you to <u>stop it</u>! He paid a great price for you. You do not have the right to put down, condemn, or punish yourself. You can begin today to see yourself as Yahweh sees you. Holy Spirit can help you.

Stay humble realizing that you cannot do this on your own. I highly recommend that you begin reading the Bible and other Christian books. Destiny Image Publishers has some good books you can read. I also recommend listening to sermons from godly teachers. I personally like Louie Giglio, Heidi Baker, Randy Clark, Beth Moore, and Mark Virkler; just to name a few. I also recommend attending Christian church services and/or conferences.

Holy Spirit will complete His work and He will take us willingly through the process. We take the action steps He leads us to take while believing in faith that He will complete His plans and purpose in and through us.

Keep in mind that Jesus is our covering. All that was needed to be done has already been done. We can rest in His finished work. Jesus is the Way, the Truth, and Life - John 14:6. He is the Light of the world, and when we follow Him, we don't have to walk in darkness - John 8:12. In Psalm 104:1-2 we see that Yahweh is covered in honor, majesty, and light. Darkness or evil doesn't coexist with Light. There is no evil in Yahweh.

Let's take this a step further - our words have creative power. They will create blessings or curses. We will harvest what we plant - Galatians 6:7. Therefore, shouldn't we choose our words more carefully? Don't we realize that all we say is (in a way) a 'prayer?' If we speak negative words, we will find ourselves spiritually 'uncovered' and in a battle.

When Adam and Eve sinned, they realized they were naked (uncovered). They tried to cover themselves with fig leaves - Genesis 3:7. Yahweh then made clothing from animal skins to clothe them - Genesis 3:21. Noah's nakedness was revealed by Ham (his son) who then exposed Noah's shame to Shem and Japeth (his older brothers). They, in turn, covered Noah without looking at him. Noah cursed Ham's son (Canaan). I read that story and thought "that kind of looks like a generational curse."

Let me try to connect the dots... We can cover one another's faults or failures by not exposing them to others. Furthermore, we can speak positive words about others. This is especially important in a marriage. Yahweh considers the husband and wife as one flesh - Mark 10:8. To hurt or expose the one is to hurt or expose the other. To uncover one's 'nakedness' brings a curse on them, their marriage; it can even travel down their generational line. I learned this by recently walking through a life lesson...

While speaking to a friend of mine, I 'uncovered' Terry when I complained about the little he had done the past weekend. I expressed my frustration in unflattering terms and ways. I see now that I spoke curses and not blessings. As soon as I realized this, I called my friend and confessed. I denounced the negative words spoken, then spoke words of blessings over Terry. Jane also recently 'uncovered' her husband by speaking negative words about him.

It seems very easy to mummer, complain, and speak negatively while to speak positively takes some effort. We must be very careful not to speak negative words (curses). We are to think and speak things that are true, honest, just, pure, love, and of good report - Philippians 4:8.

I believe we are on the cusp of a new season where Yahweh is causing an alignment. He will begin to flow through each of us in the original way He intended. He is bringing us back to the Garden of Eden (His Presence of great pleasure). In this process, He places us where He wants and brings people into our lives as He designs.

In this new season (with fall just around the corner), I sense a stirring in the air. The fall season is full of wonderful colors, smells, and cool air. I'm reminded that in Genesis 3:8 the word cool means: wind, breath, mind, spirit, Holy Spirit [1]. This is a season of renewal and eventual transformation. First comes dying to the old. Just as leaves change colors, die and fall to the ground, we must let go of our old ways.

NOTE

[1] H7307 - ruwach - Strong's Hebrew Lexicon (KJV). Retrieved from https://www.blueletterbible.org//lang/Lexicon/Lexicon.cfm?Strongs=H7307&t=KJV

NICODEMUS

I would like to share a bit of a friend's story. I do this with full permission from her...

Joy grew up in a broken family, where addiction, adultery, and some forms of abuse were the norm. Threads of fear and insecurity were woven into the very fabric of who she perceived herself to be. However, she was not created for those terrible things. Why did those things happen? Why didn't she know Yahweh during her formative years?

We all are born into a 'fallen' world. When we first arrive, we are innocent and helpless. Yes, Yahweh knows all that we will face. He designs us in Heaven then He forms (creates) us in our mother's womb. He is not at fault for the choices the parents (or others) make. Yahweh is not the orchestrator of evil.

I've wondered many times why we couldn't just stay in Heaven instead of having to enter this world. This world is full of sin, sickness, death, poverty, and evil. Why did we even have to come here? Can we stop for one second and imagine ourselves from Yahweh's perspective?

Yahweh's love is selfless, unconditional, and all encompassing. He wants relationships, not robots. He desires that we choose Him. I do not know why that decision is harder for some than for others.

At first glance, you'd think Joy was set up for failure. Or maybe you'd think she simply had a huge disadvantage. She grew up knowing nothing (good) about Yahweh. She didn't attend any church services when she was younger. All she did know is what she saw when KKK marched past her house.

What we learn in childhood will play out in our adulthood. It's familiar territory we remain in, as that is all we know. Anything opposite of what is familiar just seems wrong. Take Joy, for example, her father cheated on her mother and made Joy his confidant. He took her to bars and showed her how drinking and cigarettes were the 'normal' thing to do.

On top of all that, Joy did not experience or feel <u>real</u> love from her parents or anyone else. She was told lie after lie, such as you do not matter', 'you're not good enough' and 'you'll never amount to anything.' The lies tried to destroy her true identity. Hurtful spoken words break our spirits. Certain actions can also break one's spirit <u>and</u> cause deep wounds in the soul. Even inaction can cause great harm. For example, one could be sexually abused, tell their mother, and the mother could call the child a liar and do nothing to help the child.

Do we blame Yahweh for the lies or abuse? Some people reason in their minds that He could have stopped it. Or they think He abandoned them in those hardest of times. These people do not know Yahweh is pure love and He cannot lie. They don't realize that He was with them and experienced everything they experienced. They don't see how Yahweh leads all of us to freedom.

Most would blame the perpetrators for the harm they bring. Certainly, they are the ones physically doing the wrong things. Do you ever consider the fact that hurting people will hurt people? Not that this is an excuse! But we must look deeper. We don't really wrestle (struggle, fight) with people. The true culprit is the enemy of our souls. We have a very real enemy, satan, who has a whole spiritual army. They are rulers, authorities, powers of this dark world, and spiritual forces of evil in the Heavenly realms - Ephesians 6:12. The dark forces of evil will set people up to be hurt, who then, in turn, hurt others. The enemy (all of them) work tirelessly in an attempt to destroy us. They whisper lies into people's thoughts. Those people often act on those thoughts. And the damage goes on and on.

Joy was the enemy's punching bag for way too many years. She experienced horrific tragedies. One such tragedy was when her son was killed. He was pushed off a bridge by a group of boys who knew he could not swim. That event (orchestrated by satan himself) was one meant to take Joy out of this life as well. Satan knows that Joy is a <u>real</u> threat to his kingdom of darkness.

When her son was murdered, Joy turned to the old and familiar addiction to numb herself from the emotional turmoil. This shut her down and shut her away. It was as though the enemy stuffed her in the prison cell of narcotics, self-loathing, sorrow, depression, and fear. But he forgot that Jesus already did the work to set us all free! Jesus has the keys to unlock every prison cell door.

It took quite a while for Joy to learn the truth. The path she had to take was not an easy one! She even tried to commit suicide a number of times. The final time landed her in a psychiatric ward. That is where she first became aware of Jesus and a better way to navigate this life. Of course, the enemy didn't give up. But at that exact point in time and in that specific space, Joy got a taste of the well-springs of life. She may not have realized it back then, but she was traveling a new path, and she was not going to go down without a fight. She began seeking the Lord, going to church services, reading the Bible, and praying. The enemy fought back with the familiar addiction. He is a formidable foe, but he really had lost the war.

Joy and I met in 2012. I observed her battles, but at that time I was fighting my own skirmishes. Still, Yahweh kept putting her and me in the same space. While I saw what the addiction was doing to her, I had no idea how to help her. I believe though in many ways we helped each other in those early years of our individual spiritual journeys.

Yahweh used many other people and events to help Joy to discover Who He is and who He created her to be. She shared with me one particular event.

It was an evening service when Joy stood in line for prayer. The whole time she stood there, she was praying asking Yahweh for the minister (who is also a prophet) not to talk about generational curses because she didn't understand that. The first thing he said as he placed his hand on her head was "Lord, break the generational curse." Before she could even say 'here we go again', she landed on the floor. Someone covered her with a prayer cloth. Her body began to feel hot. An immediate super bright, super-hot light shined on her. At least, that is what she first thought.

The light was actually inside of her wanting to pour out of her. She tried to squeeze her eyes open, and it literally felt like fire balls were shooting out of her eyes. But, Yahweh wanted the light to remain inside of her. Time was irrelevant, and she had no idea how long she remained in that space.

When she finally <u>was</u> able to stand, it felt like she floated out of the building and all the way home. When she arrived at home, her husband was on the phone. She soon fell asleep and slept like she hadn't in a long time. The next few days she had to walk down a difficult path, but this time she had the Light of the Lord within her.

Days went by and she did stumble for a short while, as she returned to narcotics a few times. But the Lord wasn't done with His work. He really had broken the generational curse, but now He was in the process of removing the narcotic addiction. Joy was greatly challenged when she discovered her husband's infidelity. She queried the Lord, "why am I still here?" He said, "be still and know that I Am." Yahweh still had much work to do in order to heal her old wounds. One major wound was the loss of her son.

It just so 'happened' that at that exact same time, Yahweh was working a healing in me. I was in the process of dealing with the loss of two babies I'd aborted when I was young. (Yes, I'd been forgiven, had forgiven, and did other work necessary to process this.) Holy Spirit caused Joy and me to meet at the river. It was a beautiful sunny day, so we walked down a nature trail to a creek. We sat on a log and I shared with her the hard process I was in. She stated that she just wasn't ready to deal with the loss of her son. I encouraged her to trust Holy Spirit to help her.

Our conversation was interrupted by two young men. They stood near us and chatted with us for a bit. I gave each of them a prophetic word of knowledge and encouragement. Just as they were getting ready to walk away, I asked them their names. They were Matthew and Elijah!!! Joy and I were amazed!

A few days after the river meeting, Joy found herself in a struggle. She decided to go for a ride in her car. She 'suddenly' found herself at the bridge where her son had been killed. She doesn't recall the drive there. I teased her and said she was transported. As she sat at the crossroads (literally and spiritually), she was given a choice... stay and process her loss or turn around and go back the way she came. Yahweh gave her the courage to stay. Through the process, she was healed of that deep and sore wound! And she was healed from the narcotics addition at the same time! Praise the Lord!!

Just two months later, her husband discovered he had stage four colon cancer. He was given only 4-8 months to live. Joy realized he needed to know who Yahweh really is. She settled in her heart to remain with him throughout his journey.

There is one most interesting detail of this story I've not yet shared. The name of the bridge is Nicodemus. In the Bible Nicodemus was a Pharisee, a ruler of the Jews. He questioned Jesus about being born again. Jesus told him: "unless one is born of water and of the Spirit, he cannot enter the Kingdom of God" (John 3:5 NKJV). To be born of water means to be born physically (think of how a woman's water breaks). Jesus was saying that it wasn't enough to be born a Jew. I believe He was pointing out that we _must_ be born into this world. We likewise must be born again from Holy Spirit. When we accept Jesus as Lord and Savior, Holy Spirit comes in and begins His process of changing us. Please know: Jesus was not saying that you must be baptized in water in order to get to Heaven! John baptized in water, but Jesus baptizes with Holy Spirit - Matthew 3:11, Mark 1:7-8, John 1:33.

Nicodemus was one who stood up for Jesus. Nicodemus pointed out that it wasn't legal to convict a man without a hearing - John

7:50-51. And he was the one who bought the mixture of myrrh and aloe (about 75 pounds worth) which was used for Jesus' burial - John 19:39. So, what's the big deal? What are the connections?

Well in Joy's story, Nicodemus was basically a bridge over troubled water - where Holy Spirit completed her healing. In a sense, she was born again. For Joy, it was Jesus who stood up for her. He helped her see that she wasn't condemned to that old prison cell. Jesus' death, burial, and resurrection applied to Joy's life in a unique way.

Joy was led to the bridge that day, she walked down to the water where her son was killed, and she laid the aching to rest. Her great loss was healed, it was released in that water. After she walked back to her car, she looked in the mirror. This was the first time in 15 years (ever since her son died) that she could look in the mirror. She sat there for at least 45 minutes looking into her eyes but seeing Yahweh's love.

Of course, she remembers her son. Of course, she loves him still. But she no longer suffers. Her son's death and her loss are no longer the catalysts for addiction. Furthermore, Joy has been able to release forgiveness for those responsible for her son's death. She is really and truly free.

I know Joy well, I know that her heart is for others to be set free. She would tell you that it's not just the addiction that needs to be released. She'll say that unforgiveness is like drinking poison expecting it to kill the one who hurt you. You see forgiveness <u>must</u> be <u>released</u>. Holding it inside of you is to hold yourself captive.

In addition, every wound inside us needs to be healed. Some wounds take longer and require more balm. We must submit every lie to the Truth of the Word - what is written and spoken by Yahweh. If we hang onto the lie, we will remain in bondage.

Joy continues to walk through the process in her own spiritual journey. She hopes to help others find their own path to freedom. Joy's husband was able to see Yahweh in his life. He was completely healed from a burst appendix and the stage four colon cancer. Praise Jesus! Unfortunately, (as of the date this book was published) cancer has returned to Brad's body in a different form. Many are standing in faith via prayer that Brad will be healed again. Even more importantly, we stand in faith that Brad will reconnect with Yahweh in a deeper way.

THE HEART'S CONDITION

Just the other day as I left the grocery story, I noticed a peculiar exchange between an elderly woman and man. They were screaming at each other. I didn't pay attention to their words. But by the tone of their voices, I could tell they were very angry with each other. I wondered if this was how they acted all the time. Sadly, I've been observing many instances of people speaking unkind words or just being rude to others. Stories about people abusing or killing others have flooded my Facebook wall. Seriously, it seems like the world has gone crazy. What is WRONG with people? Maybe the answer to that question begins in the heart…

I am not referring to the physical heart, even though it can have its own issues. For instance, in mid-April of 2016, I had a small hiccup with my heart. A general surgeon had tried to biopsy a 'hot' thyroid nodule. Thyroid hormones filled my body, and I ended up in the Emergency Department with a heart rate of 120bpm. It took a month or more to regulate my heart and thyroid! Anyway, back to the spiritual/emotional heart…

Out of the heart, the mouth speaks - Proverbs 4:24, Matthew 12:34, Luke 6:45. Basically, when we speak, we are in essence exhibiting what is in our heart. Yes, we can speak out of our mind (our head knowledge). We can cite facts and figures without ever engaging our heart.

What happens when we reveal what is going on inside of us. One can actually 'bare' their soul and share their spirit with another person. When done in a positive way, we will encourage or edify another person. However, sometimes words will sting and can leave deep wounds inside of the other person. Too often people don't pay closer attention to what's really going on inside of them. Too often people aren't concerned how their words affect someone else.

Think about that elderly couple who thought nothing of revealing their heart's wounds. Their wounds probably ran deep; their hearts were clearly damaged. I'm not even sure they realized what they were doing. Could they even begin to understand that death and life are in the power of the tongue - Proverbs 18:21a? And those who love it (the tongue - well actually what they are saying) will eat its fruits (pay the consequences) - Proverbs 18:21b. What we say, we will ultimately experience. We create (by our words) the atmosphere around us.

Look at Matthew 21:22 - if we have faith (believe) we can speak (ask) and we will receive. If we believe negative, we say negative; therefore we get negative. The same is true of the positive. Imagine if that couple didn't have wounded hearts. How would their interaction have looked that day? Yes, we all lose our temper now and again. We all get frustrated, irritated, upset, or angry. But the key - the real secret to dealing with those emotions that rise inside of the heart, is to stop for a minute, recognize what is happening, and ask "where is that coming from?" We can help others process those emotions as well. Terry and I have been trying to do this for one another.

Every time I go to the doctors, the nurse will check my physical heart's condition (blood pressure and pulse). Perhaps we should give our spiritual/emotional heart a checkup as well. This could be done even before an issue arises. Yet, it definitively should be done when feelings come to the surface. We can search our heart to discern how it got that way. We can ask Holy Spirit to dig deeper to help us to see if there is an old issue or wound. We can ask Him to reveal, heal, repair, restore, and renew that area. Think of it this way: when the body has a wound, and it is not cared for, it can fester, get infected and cause serious illness - even death. The same is true of a wound in the spirit or soul. Wounds must be dealt with!

Why do most resist this process? Why do they stay stuck? Most times it's because that place (of thinking negatively) feels 'familiar' (a spirit). It just doesn't feel 'natural' to search, ask for revelation, forgive, let go of control, and allow Holy Spirit to complete the process. To do these things aren't natural, they are "super" natural – beyond what we could normally physically do.

I issue a challenge... the next time (and there will be a next time) you feel anger, frustration, or fear rise inside of you, will you try to discern what the real problem is? I pray that I can do this. I pray that all of us allow Holy Spirit to repair our heart's condition. I pray we all find forgiveness and freedom! I pray we all speak words of kindness, love, edification, and encouragement to others.

NOODLE STICK PRAYERS

I want to write what I've learned, well... still am learning. I share willingly as I know that this lesson is not just for me.

It begins with realizing who my earthly dad was and who he was not. It's accepting that he too had broken pieces, and he had no knowledge of how to relate to one such as me. It is a difficult image to view. According to my sisters, he not only related to them, he connected with them (at least in conversation). Why them and not me? I am not sure what part I played in the disconnected relationship I had with my dad. I suppose it's possible that my memory fails me. Maybe I am not recalling important details. He should (or could) have been a good representation of my Heavenly Father.

Since the memories of my childhood are very few, I can catch only a glimpse of a time or two. A few other memories are added upon viewing the memories of my teenage years into my early twenties. In those years (at least), my mother's words exposed my dad's faults and failures (just like Ham who exposed Noah's nakedness). In truth, those negative words were curse words that brought shame and degradation to my dad. Those words set up walls in her heart and mine. I picture those walls made up of thick blocks. They are covered in slippery moss and vines. Underneath all that, each block has harsh words carved into them. Those words basically translated into stay away, don't touch, don't climb. It's as if the walls held poisonous words, yet there really isn't any danger at all. The moss and vines are unpleasant to look at; they lend no comfort or assurance. It is sad, now knowing who I am. I could have truly known my dad back then, had the walls not been built or if I'd been given even half a chance. Love is a complex thing. Love's not just a feeling; love is an action and a commitment. I would have liked a better opportunity to see a deep love form between my earthly dad and me. Weird how that relationship affected and even stunted my relationship with my Heavenly Father.

I remember how awkward it was to approach my earthly dad. Once scene comes to mind… I was a teenager and walked up to him to ask for $5, so I could go to the movies or get something. I put my hand out and tried to act silly to get past the awkwardness. He smiled and gave it to me. I can clearly picture him; I even remember his scent - of cigarette smoke (even though he might have quit smoking by that point). I recall the roughness of his hands, worn that way by years of farming and carpentry work. But mostly, I remember that feeling: as if I approached a stranger or at best an acquaintance. It is the <u>strangest</u> feeling. And because I felt that way, a disconnection and lack of real relationship was my reality back then. We had no heart to heart talks. We never got to really know one another.

The natural life mirrors the spiritual life or vice versa. The relationship I had with my earthly dad is how I had perceived the relationship with my Heavenly Father. It was awkward when I approached either of them. With both, I didn't share open communication. Thankfully, Yahweh wooed me back to His heart. He restored what I had thought was lost (or what I didn't know I even had). He's helped me to truly know Him as a <u>good</u> Father.

However, if I 'forget" about our relationship and offer up a noodle stick (hit or miss) prayer, it will not avail much. Just picture throwing a cooked noodle at the wall to see if sticks (you do this to know if it's completely cooked). Upon release, just before it hits the wall, you don't know if it will stick or not.

Thankfully, we don't have to throw prayers up in the air while wondering if Yahweh hears us. Our relationship with Him is secure, and the way to Him is easy. We simply and openly talk with Him. Even though He already knows what I'm thinking and experiencing, it helps me to talk with Him about everything. I suppose this is what to 'pray without ceasing' means - 1 Thessalonians 5:17.

I can only imagine the struggle my oldest daughter must be having in relation to her father's suicide. Their relationship was tenuous at best. He was never an easy man for her (or I) to get along with while she was growing up. I wish I could say words that would take her hurt away. I wish she didn't have to go through this. I wish I could travel back in time to help him heal and prevent his meanness to her. I wish I could have warned him and he could have avoided his accident. I wish he would have made a better effort to love her like a daddy should. Even though I know he tried to love her the only ways he knew how I wish he'd learned a better way before she came along. I wish I could have prevented his tragic death. Alas, my wishes cannot come true.

So instead I simply love her through the valley of grief. Grief is many layered and makes little sense to the mind. But somehow the heart takes the path and finds its way. You must let grief ebb and flow as it wills. Sometimes it's angry and other times sad. It can be denial or even acceptance.

My prayer is that both my daughters discover the freedom of

open communication with our Heavenly Father. I hope they learn the art of real prayer instead of the noodle stick kind. Yahweh has so much to offer us.

Recently, He showed me (in the spirit) an umbrella with each section a different color, but each has certain flavors and scents. He is our covering, and when we step under the umbrella, we obtain all He has for us. He desires close relationship with us. He wants to share His heart with us. He's not interested in religious (noodle stick) prayers. He wants to share our lives with us!

IT IS FINISHED

I do not know why things happen the way they do. Why is there sickness, pain, suffering, poverty, and death in this world? Even in my questioning, I honestly believe the Bible is true. The promises in the old covenant were met by Christ, in the new covenant. By His stripes (wounds) we are healed, and He was pierced for our transgressions - Isaiah 53:5. He was delivered over to death for our trespasses and was raised to life for our justification - 1 Corinthians 15:3-4, Hebrews 9:28, 1 Peter 2:24. While on the cross Jesus said, "It is finished." He returned to Heaven, and Holy Spirit dwells inside of us. So quite literally all that needed to be done has been done. Considering these truths, why do people still struggle with illness or with each other?

Speaking of struggle, my first EEG test showed some abnormality. Thus I had to complete a 48-hour EEG test. This involved having wires attached to my scalp. I wore them to the RV show in Hershey, PA. I joked with Terry that I was an avatar. I don't know how I was taking that experience lightly. Later, that same day, Lindsey texted me - her husband was suicidal, he had left work, and she couldn't locate him. I felt helpless but couldn't allow myself to run around in a panic. Instead, I talked with Yahweh and asked Him to intervene.

Around this the same timeframe, I noticed some other people struggling with their lives and relationships. One person commented that she didn't deny Jesus existed, but she denies

He's the only Way to Heaven. I wish I could show her how to flip that around. I wish she could realize that there was NO way to Heaven, but He made the Way. I can't convince anyone of Jesus' works or even of Who He really is. All I can do is share what I have experienced, how I know Him, and that I have seen Holy Spirit presently active in my life.

Anyway... I received the second EEG test results which showed normal brain activity. I got my driver license back the same day I received the documentation. A few days later, Terry and I went away for a short work trip. It seemed like troubles surrounded me and I felt rubbed raw emotionally and mentally. It was a relief to get some time away. On the way to the site, Terry's truck tire blew. Instead of getting stressed out, I was just glad it didn't cause an accident.

After we got back from our trip, Lindsey told me that Nick was talking about divorce. I wanted to cry and wail but that never helps. My mind ran to and fro, searching for solutions. The emotions of concern, sadness, worry, and anger filled my chest. Questions pounded my soul - what will happen? How will they survive? I sort through my memories - what did I do, how did I survive? Where did I find safety and security? What safe haven did I nest in? My questions seemed stupid and faithless to me. But Yahweh didn't condemn me for the asking of them. He knew what was going on and already had the answer in place. I released the worry into His capable Hands and asked Him to give my daughter (and me) peace during this storm. I'm sure we all grow weary of walking through storms. It's exhausting and I, for one, detest the process.

A few days after the trip, I met my brother, Scott, at Paul's old trailer to do the final clean out. Terry hadn't planned on coming to help but finally did. Lindsey came down Saturday afternoon and Sunday morning. She was challenged in helping because she was pretty far along in her pregnancy. Her burden was great. She had to arrange for her dad's things to be sold. She had to make the final arrangements for his funeral. He left her with such a mess. The stress and mess made me angry at Paul (for a little while anyway). I did what I could, but it seemed very little. It made me feel somewhat panicked because I knew I wouldn't be able to solve anything.

Finally, the cleanup was finished. I went home, laid down, and watched a show about someone trying to help a woman who basically lost everything, including her identity. I wondered how this could happen. Where did she lose herself and why? I realized that her choices were made with a flawed or damaged soul, which led her to a life of abuse and squalor. She suffered from some form of mental illness and was given an offer of help. However, she remained in the lifestyle she'd chosen. I wonder what happened to her after the show.

How many women (and men) fall into this same trap. They are damaged, lose themselves, and believe they're defeated. On some level, some will see themselves as failures and they somehow deserve the horrible situation they are in. However, no one is a victim of circumstance. Choices (ours or others) lead us down the path we go. When we 'wake up' we can make new choices - - if we would just believe in ourselves and the possibilities.

Certainly, my history is filled with wrong choices and unhealthy relationships. Back then, I was thoroughly lost in depression. I'm sure I believed I had no choices. Therefore, I got exactly what I believed. I accepted what was unacceptable. Yes, I wanted out of the unhealthy relationships I'd found myself in. But old failures, wrong beliefs, and fear stymied me. I was angry and even hated myself for being weak. I didn't really know where to begin to get the complete healing I needed. I was one of the millions of women (and men) who suffer needlessly for too long.

Yes, I was a Christian and I'd seen counselors. But I didn't really know how to go about walking a spiritual walk of faith or how to form a close relationship with Yahweh. I suppose I did the best I know how to do at the time. Even though I dealt with so many issues, I was able to help raise my children. I am grateful I was able to do that.

I wonder if I could go back to my former self and share what I know now, would I believe? Perhaps I could convince myself of necessary changes. But which changes would I make? And if I managed to change my old viewpoint, would my life be different now? Alas, we cannot go back in time. I'm simply grateful that my life began to change. It was a slow process of Yahweh's healing and renewal of me. He helped me discover who I really am. He helped me to stop seeing myself as 'damaged beyond repair.' He refused to let me play the victim. He taught me what "It is finished" really looks like on a day-to-day basis. Basically, I simply trust in the finished work Jesus did. Moving forward, I wonder how I could help others learn their value. Lead on Holy Spirit...

PROPHESY

I wrote the following on 10/2/16....

It's a chilly fall morning and I came to the river to be alone with Yahweh, Jesus, and Holy Spirit. The dew on my window makes it hard to see out the side so I look ahead. The river is clear as glass and a few ducks remain on it. They glide along smoothly, it almost looks like they are skating on their bellies. I can only see so far because the mist covers the landscape in the distance. It's very quiet here. A fish just popped up out of the water, nibbling what it found on that still surface. More ducks join the few and now trails are made. Are they wandering aimlessly, or do they have a destination or purpose in mind. A few ducks dive under, getting a quick bath and I wonder - don't they feel the cold?

The days have slipped by much like the mist on the water that slowly but steadily evaporates into the air. I have not written. What have I done with my time – nay not mine, it has never been mine. This life I live belongs to Jesus - all I am, all I once perceived as mine belongs to Him.

I slipped and fell back into the natural realm as troubles not even my own have surrounded me and engulfed me. They try to swallow up the peace and joy – and I have allowed it. I cannot lie - - my attention was garnered by them. Oh how that frustrates me.

Yet, through this valley of trials and sorrows, I have (on occasion) cast my cares onto Jesus. I have cried out to Holy Spirit from my spirit, sometimes in words only He could understand. I release all of it into Yahweh's very capable hands.

Mind – I say to you: rest, abide, let go of all reasoning, planning, and control. **Emotions** – you are just energy, not right or wrong, go ahead and feel but breathe out into the heart of the Father. Allow your energy to spill onto Daddy – He knows just what to do. **Will** – you are determined and quite stubborn, even stiff necked at times. When will you see that you are not in control and hold no responsibility other than to garner all our (*the entire soul*) attention and energy back to Jesus. Truly He can do above and beyond what we are capable of –more than what we could ever hope or dream of. Run to Him, grab His warm and callused hands, they comfort us. Look into His eyes – pools of love (pure adoration). Feel the warmth of His love running like a pure river out of Him and encompassing all of us. Breathe in His scent – His life-giving Spirit. Remember what He has already done – He <u>said,</u> "It is finished."

Don't turn your focus onto the natural troubles – they hold nothing for you. Stay in His incredible, powerful, and amazing Presence. This is where you'll find grace, strength, love, and mercy. You will be able to continue one more day and take one more step. Stay here, in this moment, on this day. Don't look to the left or to the right. Don't turn your head trying to see what is back there (in history). Remember only what Yahweh, Jesus, and Holy Spirit have been doing in and through you since the beginning OF you. Yahweh designed you. He created and formed you in your mother's womb. All you should ever need was put inside of you – deep into your spiritual DNA and spiritual womb.

You can do <u>all</u> things according to the riches in Christ Jesus. You have <u>all</u> right here, right now! Do not doubt. Do not disbelieve. These only distract. JUST BELIEVE. Allow Holy Spirit to do His work deep inside of you. He is quite capable and the only One with the gifts and fruits. He gives them to us freely. Let go of the natural –the good enough and realize you have the Greater – He is the Greater and dwells inside of you. I feel that Yahweh just spoke to my heart: "*I speak to your sleepy spirit, wake up, wake up I say! I call you AWAKE. Shake off the old dusty slumber. You are a mighty warrior – trained, proven, and already perfected. Call out to Me and I shall answer you. Call out the Name above all names – JESUS!*"

Abba Daddy, thank You for this peaceful place of Your Presence. Thank You Holy Spirit for lifting that burden (of not even mine) off me and bringing me back to this beautiful reality of Your life. Certainly, I know You never held anything against me (even when I felt lost in a vortex).

THE DARKEST VALLEY

The next few stories contain actual edited excerpts from my personal journal. What I wrote was real and very emotionally raw. I feel vulnerable to share such personal things. But I hope in the sharing of this, it will help someone, somewhere. My daughter, Lindsey has given me full permission to share the stories. Out of respect for my daughter's wishes, I have not shared her children's first names. I use M for her daughter, K for her son, and J for her baby boy.

<u>10/7/16</u> - My sister called me concerned for Lindsey and her situation. It was weighty. I have been helping Lindsey with her dad's final affairs. Terry and I have had a small conflict that we worked through fairly quickly. I struggle with my limitations and feel desperate and very sad. Lord Jesus, I need You. Holy Spirit I ask for Your grace, strength, and comfort. I know and believe I was designed and created for 'greater' - please let it be. Nothing but Yahweh can satisfy. Daddy, I ask for Your promise to manifest on earth as it is in Heaven.

I realize that I must be intimately connected to Yahweh, Jesus, and Holy Spirit - be fully aligned with Them. When I pray, it needs to be from that deep intimate place of relationship with Them.

Hurricane Matthew is getting ready to hit the lower southeastern states. I thought of praying - what do I say or ask? Why do we ask the Father when He has already given us the authority, grace, gifts, and ability to do what Jesus did and even greater? How do we appropriate His power properly and effectively? Jesus said if we ask anything in His Name, He will do it so the Father may be glorified in the Son - John 14:12-14. Shouldn't I be able to command the wind to be still? Why wouldn't it obey the sound of my voice? After all, I am filled with Holy Spirit's power and Jesus' authority. What key am I missing? Am I not truly believing? It is the will of the Father for us to have abundant life. He cannot lie. I can and do say 'Let His Kingdom come and His will be done in our lives. Holy Spirit search me - all of me. Anything that would hinder Your work - remove, repair and redeem!'

10/3/16 – Lindsey texted with me wondering about a place to go if she needed it (for a few days). Now I know that Nick had been staying at his mother's house a lot. It was such a heavy burden that I could tangibly feel. She then asked me to watch the kiddos because Nick had an appointment with a psychiatrist. When I got there, Nick was asleep on the couch with M beside him. I asked her where mommy was. She told me that K had taken too much medicine and they went to the doctors. I woke Nick up and he explained in a tad more detail. Soon he left to go to his appointment, and I stayed with M. He wasn't gone long. When he got back, I talked with him about my medical history. I shared more details than he had known before. It was clear that he was struggling. I asked him about the medicine check and told him to be careful weaning on and off them. He said he couldn't understand why he wasn't happy, he had a wife who loved him unconditionally, fairly healthy kids, a home, a good job...

I told him that things outside of us can't make us happy. We have to find it inside us and only God can help us with that. I told him to talk to God about it all, that it's okay to vent. Yes, He knows all, but it helps us. Then we need to let Him get inside us and fix it. I then spoke about how I went off prescription medications, but this isn't for everyone. He said, "you use your faith to help you." I soon prepared to leave. Nick laid on the love seat and M was running around. He said, "M, come give me a hug." Later I texted Nick to see how K was doing and he said he was good (or fine) and he was eating supper.

10/8/16, 6:00 a.m. – I woke with my eyes red and puffy, my face (mostly left side) red, itchy, and warm. My first thought was that I was having an allergic reaction. I took an antihistamine and tried to go back to sleep. I couldn't. I texted Nick (as he is a paramedic) with a picture to ask his advice, should I go to the ED? I hate making this call on my own. I apologized for texting him that early. He never responded.

1:39 p.m. - Lindsey called me & said: "come NOW." I prayed on the way to her house. As I prayed, I tried not to fret or imagine what might be wrong. When I arrived, she urged me to get the kids out of the house. Nick had texted a picture of a gun to her, and she didn't want the kiddos to be there. She was certain he'd never hurt any of them, but she didn't want the police showing up and the kids to see or hear anything. I was worried about her. I didn't want her there alone. She insisted she'd be fine but wanted to protect the kids. I drove around with the kiddos for a while, got Terry, went to the dollar store for stuff for them, then to my travel trailer. They had a lot of fun running around and playing with the toys I got them.

3:45 p.m. (10/8/16) - Lindsey texted me "He's gone mom" meaning Nick had died. These were the same words she'd texted me after her dad had killed himself in May. I couldn't believe it. Lindsey's friend Sequoia called me, she was on her way to Lindsey. I thank the Lord for her. Terry and I stayed with the kids in the travel trailer till we took them home around 7:45. I got them changed into their PJs and into bed. Sequoia and Lindsey had gone to get food. Lindsey texted me around 8, "how do we tell our family?" I texted back "I don't know."

10/9/16, 10:03 p.m. - How does one say goodbye to one you welcomed into your heart as a son. How do you stand when waves of grief sweep over you and land you on your knees. How does one watch their daughter cry. How do you look into the eyes of such precious little ones knowing they'll never see daddy on this earth again. How do you answer when they ask "is daddy working?" Or "when is daddy coming home?" Yahweh's grace, only by His grace. I trust Him. I still feel the grief.

10/12/16, 7:26 a.m. - How does one effectively walk the path of grief. For me – it is only by faith in Yahweh, walking beside Jesus, led and comforted by Holy Spirit. I have walked many valleys - - of sorrow and pain. I have wandered in the wilderness of testing and trial. I have faced my own death a number of times. I have cried and struggled more times than I can even count. Through it all, my Lord and Savior carried me through. And he will carry me through this time too - "Even though I walk through the valley of death, I fear no evil, for You (*my Jesus*) are with me. Your rod and staff they comfort me." (Psalm 23:4 NKJV, emphasis added)

I am very blessed to have many praying for my family and me as we mourn the death of Nick. The lives of my daughter Lindsey and their kiddos are forever changed. It is one thing to have your own struggles - I have fought through mine many times and with the Lord have won victory after victory. But to see your children and grandchildren struggle - oh my. I have no words. I only look to the Father's face. I depend on His grace. I apply it in words, feeling, and action. And I will not stop. I will fight. I am an overcomer and I will have this victory too. I will see the Father multiply His blessings for my children. I will see Him turn this tragedy to the good because He IS a good Father. I am amazed by Him.

10/12/16, 7:44 p.m. – I treasure the lovely moments. Moments of wee ones smiles or better yet giggles. Moments when my grandchildren run to me yelling "mom mom" or climb into my lap to read a book. I like when they make their mommy smile because they are being silly.

The harder moments usually hit when I am home and the wave of grief hits me out of nowhere. Or moments like when tears start in Lindsey's eyes and end in mine. Sometimes the hard moments cause a huge tsunami. It engulfs my chest till I can barely breathe. An awareness comes over me - Nick is gone. A deep breath of disbelief fills my lungs as I gasp for air.

We all are trying to find a new normal. It's like looking for a black cat in a dark room. Time has become even more precious to me. I give freely to Lindsey and the wee ones. Although, I need to dedicate time to Angelica and her wee ones too. Why does it seem like it has been months since I've seen them? Angelica has told me not to worry about it so much. Why is time so weird?

I cling to the love. I cling to my faith. I cling to the beauty that the Lord is bringing out of the ashes. I don't know how He does it, but He does. I have seen such kindness - - heartfelt acts of kindness.

It has proven to me (and I think to Lindsey) that love reigns strong still.

10/13/16, 7:43 a.m. - I would like to know where "normal" went. I've tried to find it, but it got lost in some foggy haze somewhere. Not very long ago (a week, two... again time is weird) a prophet told Terry and I that we were entering a new season. I was beyond ready for it. I couldn't have imagined how this season would begin. Would I have tried to run from it or tried to prevent it in some way? Is there anything any of us can do? Maybe just learn... learn how precious life is. Slow down, be patient and kind to others. We don't know what battles another person is fighting. Many couldn't have seen the struggles Nick faced every stinking day. Most don't know the day to day life another one lives. When we open our eyes to see others (even in the middle of our storms), deep inside most carry love. I'm finding this truth in some unusual places, with people I'd not really looked closely at before. Yesterday it was the dental hygienist. All the times before, we shared surface talk and she was always nice. This time, as I couldn't help but share my heart, she was extraordinarily kind. The story I shared may have made her go home and hug her family a little tighter and love them a little deeper.

I've heard others tragic stories before. While I felt for those involved, I really couldn't fully understand or relate. My choice would have been NOT to be able to. Yet going through this has made me much more aware --- of everything and everyone.

As a Christian seer, I thought I was in tune. But this time, this season, this event, has tuned my vision even more than I could have thought possible. I've become so much more aware of the deep abiding love my Heavenly Father has for me, for all of us.

That love is rich, full, alive, breathing, pulsing... His heart beat - beats somehow in my chest. His love somehow becomes mine, which I give freely to my daughters and their families. Each day going forward, I encourage you to stay present and aware of those souls around you. Love, love, love...

GRIEF'S ANGER

10/14/16, 7:35 p.m. - Today was one of the hardest valleys I've ever had to walk through. And I don't quite know how to process all the levels of grief. I've never been good at processing anger, and now it has all these shades of colors (sadness, frustration, irritation, disbelief...). At first, I managed the grief well when I watched the wee ones while they played this morning. This was before they realized their little worlds had changed. But necessary words had to be spoken by their mommy before another person said them. As M listened (while she tried to block the flow of words no child should have to hear), I watched the grace in Lindsey. I saw her tears first then heard M cry as she looked up at her daddy's picture. I shared my tears as well, which fell harder when that little girl touched her mommy's face and tried to wipe the tears and the words away. How does a three-year-old know how to comfort.

After a few moments I suggested a walk for me and the wee ones; we all needed to regroup. As soon as we lost sight of the house, M shared her little heart with me. It was as if she waited on purpose because she didn't want to cause her mommy any more discomfort. The grace she already has! Later in the walk, it was K who told a neighbor "daddy, Heaven." This is something a two-year-old should never have to say.

Later, I was upstairs and the sound machine in the kiddos room was on (both the light & sound). The wee ones I suspected. I went in, turned it off, walked out and shut the door. Immediately both came back on again. I recall it being on earlier too. I've debated sharing this news. I don't quite know what to make of it. I've got many questions. I do know that if Nick could reach this realm from Heavens realm, this is a prank he would pull. But I cannot find any humor in it.

Then as I put some clothes away, I saw something that reminded me of the struggle Lindsey and Nick had while she was pregnant with M (K somewhat too). An unexpected wave hit me. Anger came, along with such tiredness. I'm angry, oh so <u>very</u> angry. I'm angry that any of this happened at all. I'm angry these precious children won't fully know their daddy. I'm angry that many of their questions won't have answers. I'm angry he won't be here for their milestones. I know the importance of a daddy in a child's life. And I'm angry he won't be here to provide that. I'm angry that others must help pick up the pieces. I'm angry at the illness. I'm angry at whatever troubles were involved or led up to them. I'm angry that my daughter has to navigate this harsh valley of grief, questions, pain, suffering, and more. I'm angry that the world lost a good man, one who had much to offer to it. I want to scream until my throat bleeds.

And (sigh), yes, I am angry at Nick. I really don't want to be. I have great empathy for him as I too have walked the path of mental illness. As I fought the battles, I pictured my daughter's faces and by Yahweh's grace, I remained. Sometimes I still must fight those battles. These days I see their faces along with my grandchildren's faces. Still, I remain. I would walk through a valley of fire for them; I already have.

While I understand Nick's struggle, it hurts that he couldn't do the same. How have I survived when many others haven't? I don't have many answers, except...

Pure grace - my faith in Jesus along with the protection and comfort of Holy Spirit. Of course, all these are available to everyone. But not everyone realizes what's there, right in front of them. We have an open door with free access, it is available here and now. We don't have to wait till we step onto the other side.

I'm angry that religion has turned many away from the love. I'm angry when hurting people hurt others. I'm angry that hurt, misunderstanding, or whatever distracts us from Who Yahweh really is. I'm angry that people are not loving and kind toward one another and I know that hurts Yahweh's heart. When will the evil, sorrow, meanness, and hurt end?

Just after I wrote the above, Pastor Rob called me. He was very encouraging and assured me that Yahweh will turn this to the good as we know the heart of the Father – His very nature and character is kind, gentle, and full of love. He even mentioned beauty for ashes.

GRATITUDE

10/14/16, 8:11 p.m. - The director from the funeral home texted me. He had decided he was going to take care of all the charges for Nick's cremation. She won't have to pay anything. He said, "She is such a quality young lady, and she needs some breaks right now." I immediately became overwhelmed by the incredible, beautiful love of Abba Daddy. I am undone. Laughing and crying at the same time, I'm barely able to breathe. I know Daddy did this through that man, for my daughter and for me to see. My mind can't wrap around the ideas. It simply accepts them as the spiritual reality of Yahweh's Kingdom.

Last week during the worship service I called Heaven to earth – His Kingdom come, His will be done. What creative words – Yahweh created what came out of my mouth. The blessing was already real in Yahweh's realm – more than I can even imagine. But Yahweh manifested His reality in this natural reality.

Earlier today, when I left my daughter's home, I was exhausted (physically, mentally, emotionally). I could take no more grief this day. While I could feel how Holy Spirit's Presence covered me like a warm cloak (all day yesterday and today). Still, I was weary. And I couldn't see how I could go one more moment let alone one more day. The funeral director, in Yahweh's kindness, was able to lift some of that burden. I can't describe the beauty….

10/15/16, 7:55 p.m. - How can I even express the gratitude for those who answered a prayer that I cried out to Yahweh. My prayer was simple - for people to show my daughter Christ's love in action. The answers came in many forms, from many different people. It even came from those who don't know or ascribe to Christianity. Everyone has the ability to love. How amazing - the visits, prayers, giving to the fund, bringing food to Lindsey and the wee ones. So much love!

I am incredibly humbled and grateful for every act of kindness, service, donation, and prayer given to Nick's family. All of us get to see Jesus' love in action every day, every hour, every moment. I am blessed when someone blesses me. But oh, when someone blesses one of my children - oh my. I have no words. All I know to say is "thank you and may Yahweh bless each one above and beyond what they could ever imagine or hope for."

This afternoon, I went to the store and was going to hang up a flier (about the fund raising) that I had made. My sleep deprived brain couldn't find the bulletin board. I got a few groceries and left. I went to my husband's bank then to the gas pumps - 30 cents off (sweet!). At first, I didn't know why I did things in that order.

A man was on the other side of the pump. He talked with me, then I shared the story and gave him the flier. He told me his son talked about killing himself not long ago. And that he has been able to be there for his son. I told him I was glad that he was and to always to take such a statement seriously. We talked about how the stigma is slowly lifting off mental illness. He almost couldn't believe the timing and the "chance encounter." But he seemed to understand how Yahweh works. He opened his wallet and gave me the few dollars that remained there. He said that I'd blessed him by sharing my daughter's story. Kindness reigned today from a complete stranger to me. I gave the money and the story to Lindsey.

Psalm 56:8 basically says that Yahweh keeps track of our sorrows, He collects our tears and stores them in a bottle. I probably need a bigger bottle in Heaven for all the ones I have shed. Are there different bottles for different types of tears? Or all tears the same there?

Someday Jesus will wipe away our tears and there will be no more death, mourning, crying, or pain - Revelation 21:4. I look forward to that. This world holds entirely too much of these things. And unfortunately, the enemy is the root cause, but humans play a part. How lovely it would be if we could all be like that stranger I met today. How amazing if we could simply smile, slow down, let someone else go first, share a kind word or two, or bless another in some small way.

Certainly, Nick knew (and still knows) the love people have for him. Love multiplies when it is given to those around us. I wish love could have healed Nick's mind while he was here. He is healed now and I am thankful for that. I am thankful for the healing process which occurred from this loss. Healing is slowly taking place in all who knew Nick. I'm incredibly amazed at how such a tragic event has brought an open awareness to mental illness. Maybe one day, in this world, the stigma will be gone completely. It doesn't exist in Heaven. I call Heaven to earth. Yahweh's Kingdom come, His will be done on earth as it is in Heaven. Amen

10/16/16, 7:17 p.m. - Today my body is feeling the effects of the stress, strain, and grief. My soul is tired and weary. My spirit abides in Jesus. I want to do more, be more. I want the greater things - John 14:12-14. My human flesh frustrates me. I must remind myself I'm only one small part of the body of Christ. I'm only one bit of humanity. I'm not meant to do it all.

There was a time I acted as if I was super woman. I overworked this frail flesh and instead of leaping tall buildings in a single bound, I smashed into them. I was the one who went tumbling down. It has taken years for me to learn the warning signs for when I'm approaching the end of my strength. In the past, I pushed past the point of my human endurance and ended up ill and flat on my back. I've had many hard uphill climbs. I would push, pull, and struggle. I'd only land worse off than before. I'd cry and beat myself up for not doing or being more. It used to be that I only saw my failures and I hadn't yet learned the secret. I did not see the promise hidden in the problem. I thank the Lord that I can now experience gratitude.

LITTLE BOATS

I have willingly walked through many deep valleys. I can't and don't walk alone anymore. I picture the village full of love for Lindsey and her wee ones. It's humbling, refreshing, and amazing. Oh my, to know that I can let go and other people will help. It's wonderful to know that we are not alone in this journey. I think of a story I discovered not too long ago. It was a story I'd just happened to stumble upon at a time Joy had a great need. And today it spoke to me. I ask all who read this to bear with me as I try to explain.

The story is found in Mark 4:35-41. Jesus told His disciples they were going to cross over the sea to the other side. It was a prophetic promise, but they probably didn't understand that. They got into the boat and began the journey. Here's the surprise that I found for Joy, and it applies to Lindsey's current situation: other little boats were in the water besides the boat Jesus was in.

When I first read the story and saw the little boats, I had some questions. Where did they come from? Why are they there? Why didn't I see them before?

So, there they all were, and a storm hit. This was not any small squall. This was a nor'easter. It didn't seem to faze Jesus, but it terrified the disciples. And four of them were seasoned fisherman. I'd imagine those four had seen their share of storms.

I've heard that many dangerous storms happened on the Sea of Galilee. But this storm must have been a doozy. So, if the fisherman were freaking out, what about the people in the other little boats? I know I would have freaked out! I do not like storms, but my daughters do. To my chagrin, my daughters used to like to brave danger running outside in the storm.

Jesus used His authority to stop the wind and calm the sea. The result was immediate. It's wild to think that He didn't prevent the storm. Why? Was there a lesson for those in that storm? Isn't there one for us as well? We can apply this same story to our lives now, today.

Did everyone in that storm see the promise and the miracle? Do we see them today? When we are in our own storm, do we notice the other little boats that come alongside us? Do we realize that we carry the authority of Jesus within us?

Right now, Lindsey is in a nor'easter. I see Jesus' love in the people who have come alongside her and me. What some may think are just simple acts of kindness, are really words and actions that have calmed the winds and sea. When each person gives just a little, we can see the wind cease and experience a great calm. What is your reaction when a storm hits?

The disciples were in awe and terribly afraid. Their minds couldn't grasp how the wind and sea obeyed Jesus. But this was normal for Jesus, He was just doing what was inside of Him to do and what He saw the Father doing. Why do we discount the miracles we see every single day?

We may think our love in action is minor. But it is the greatest thing. We too can change the atmosphere. We too can help another navigate the storm. And when it's our turn to face a storm, others can come alongside and help us too. It is what we all are meant to do.

I think too of what Jesus, the disciples, and others <u>didn't</u> do in that storm. They didn't jump into the sea. They stayed in the storm. Jesus had the ability to walk on water, but He stayed in the boat with those terrified men. He didn't feed the fear. He simply used His voice to command the wind and sea. Our words have creative power too. What do we create with what we say? Negative begets negative. Positive begets positive. Let us always speak creative, positive words to everyone. You literally can change someone's storm into quiet calm.

What if one had fallen into the water in that storm. Words wouldn't have reached their understanding in that moment. A wrong action would lead to more trouble. If I were to jump in the water trying to save a drowning person, I'd probably go under too. We need to be wise and trained. We need to know what to do. How do we learn that? In a literal drowning scenario, the only thing I think I could do is to throw out a life line or a lifebuoy. But action I'd need to take. Nick was a lifeguard, he knew how to save a drowning person. It makes me sad that it is Nick who went under this time. But his story can reach others; it can help others keep from drowning in their sea of despair.

No matter how dark someone's storm, we can show them love and support. I encourage everyone to pull up your boat alongside someone and let us see love in action.

I am bone tired and weary. My health situation isn't the best right now. The effects of stress, grief, and not caring for this frail body is catching up to me. I continue to write but can't take credit for what flows out of me. As I said before, I am simply a pen in my

Father's hand. I am grateful and in awe of how the words just come. They are deep and meaningful to me and those close to me. I am happy to be able to tell this story - one with many nuances. I want to paint a picture of sorts with Yahweh's words and exploits. I want others to catch this vision - Yahweh gives us all a dream. He has given me a dream (vision) which is much greater than I am or could hope for. I want to take a giant leap of faith and see Him fulfill it all. His plans for me are good, to give me a future and hope - Jeremiah 29:11. I trust Yahweh and find new strength. I will run and not grow weary. I will walk and not faint - Isaiah 40:31.

The enemy tried to steal, kill, and destroy - but no more! NO more I say! Yahweh prevails and carries me through each circumstance. He has healed, redeemed and restored me. He will NEVER fail. He will NEVER forsake. His love is pure and genuine. He is very beautiful indeed. He has enabled me - well He literally built me - to accomplish His plan and purpose. I give Yahweh all the glory and honor. His dream is way beyond my ability and resources. If He doesn't accomplish it, it can't and won't be done. He instilled this huge dream inside of me. At times I have gotten a glimpse here and a taste there. I look forward to seeing it come about. I imagine people standing in awe of what He has done. I pray for His Wisdom and Revelation. I ask Him to let me see every opportunity, help me to walk through each in faith and allow me to speak His Words.

I pray when people read the words I write (Yahweh's messages), they see Him. Let my entire life, every bit of me reflect Him. As the dream begins to manifest in this natural realm, may He help me to steward it well.

My dream and purpose aren't just for me - it's for others. It's meant to create a legacy. I pray others discover who they are designed to be and what they are gifted to do. Deep down in their spirits, I think people know why they are here. The enemy, distractions, doubts, unbelief, and such seem to veer people off track. It is time to speak to the potential in people - give positive words of encouragement and affirmation. We turn on the light and darkness flees. We shine the Light of Christ into deep recesses of the heart, and people come alive!

I honestly don't know how the minutes blend into hours and the hours into days. I watch Lindsey's little ones and it's hard to understand that Nick left them - he is gone, just GONE from their lives. Today M picked up a book with all their pictures in it and she cried. Then Lindsey cried. I asked M if she wanted me to hold her - she did. There will be no more pictures of her daddy, and no new memories of him with his children will be made. It makes me sad and angry all at the same time. These emotions just ebb and flow like a river of emotional energy.

Will any of us ever get accustomed to the empty place where Nick should be. There are moments when I visit their home and almost expect him to be there. I don't know how the loss of the little one's daddy will affect them long term. I pray that the men who are still in their lives will step up and fill in where they can. I pray that they have good male role models. May every one of us realize we play an important role. Sometimes we find ourselves in the big boat with Jesus. At other times we are in a little boat. And at other times we may be lost in the sea of pain, chaos or confusion. Each one of us matters - we can make a difference! Pull your boat up alongside someone today.

VALLEY OF ELAH

10/18/16 - Life became a bit overwhelming today. Stress and concern weighed heavy down upon me and this frail body could take no more. I was irritable, hungry, and tired and it showed in my actions, words, and tones towards Terry. I regret that. I finally gave in and slept. I desperately needed that nap, but I remained groggy for some time afterwards.

While my spirit remains in the realm with Holy Spirit, I still dwell in a human body with a soul. All together the effects of way too much, way too soon are felt deeply. I am amazed by Yahweh's grace. What a journey this has been.

10/21/16 - My youngest granddaughter turned one today. The day sped by and before I knew it, it was done. Time reminds me of a river - how it can move slowly or quickly depending on the season or weather. When the rushing water of time overwhelms me, it's hard to remain present in the moment. One day I will look back on this time and clearly see Yahweh's hand in each second.

It's strange to think that in the spiritual realm, time and space are not measurable. What will it be like to live fully in that realm? Or once there, will we realize we are finally home - in the place where we belong. It is our destiny after all. But I suppose while we are here, we can enjoy life, love those close to us, and make our lives count.

Many times, I've wanted Yahweh to change my circumstances, but instead, He used my circumstances to change me. Seriously though, I need to stop letting circumstances derail me. He is teaching me that I can't do this life, fulfill His plan, or accomplish any great thing on my own (within my own strength or ability). Yahweh <u>must</u> do what I cannot do, yet He works through me. He will place other people in our lives to help us at specific points for specific reasons. And each person is responsible for their own choices.

I have a sense that something is about to happen, yet I know not what. It makes me sad and anxious. I don't really like this sensation. Why do I assume it's negative. What if Yahweh's about to do something amazing. I know that He can, and I haven't forgotten all He has already done. "Now to Him who is able to do exceedingly abundantly above all that we ask or think, according to the power that works in us" (Ephesians 3:20 NKJV).

Yahweh hears my cries and He will answer my prayers. Even in this most difficult valley of grief, suffering, and in overwhelming challenges, Yahweh has given me much more than I can even describe. He has given me Terry who helps in any way he can. Yahweh's brought others to help Lindsey and to show her Christ's love in action. He has given me books to read that literally have what I need in the exact moment needed.

Just now, as I am writing, "Valley of Elah" popped into my head. Okay, what is up with that? The battle between David and Goliath happened in that valley - 1 Samuel 17:2,19; 21:9. How many giants have I faced (spiritually or naturally) - giants of sickness, finances, death, faith challenges, and more. How did David defeat the giant? He was trained in the field - he tended sheep; He fought lions and bears, and he spent time in the Presence of

Yahweh. David was a man after Yahweh's heart. I wonder at David's courage as he faced Goliath. Where did it come from? Certainly, it wasn't just human courage that caused David to rush into the valley of Elah after a man who was probably three times his size.

A giant is meant to scare, worry, distress, conquer, or defeat us. A giant (enemy) issue, problem or concern will do its best to make you think it cannot be defeated. However, we have the ability and the right (authority) to turn it around. We can spend time in Yahweh's Presence. He is our ever-present help in any problem- Psalm 46:1. Jesus is our blessed hope - Titus 2:13.

Like David, we are trained or prepared "in the field." We will face adversity and we will conquer - but not in of our own strength or ability. Yahweh provides us with what we need. He gives us the ability to stand even when we face a giant.

So... like David, I will stand. I will not turn tail and run! I am a warrior, hear me roar! I will look to Yahweh's face in great expectation. He WILL give me the victory and even greater. He will deliver, strengthen and provide for me. I shall remain true to Yahweh and to myself (all of who He created me to be). He will cause others to see what I am made of. I am not a victim of this current circumstance. I step on circumstances' throat and cut off their head. I will even use the giant's own weapon to kill it. I am a conqueror and victor because of what Jesus already did for me!

I proclaim: WE ARE NOT ALONE!! We don't face the giant alone! We are fully connected, dependent and reliant on Jesus.

We can read the written Word and hear His spoken word. Every day at any given moment we can choose to walk on His word.

As I was writing this story, Joy texted me "Can't we just ask for one day to ourselves - to do whatever we want; where we don't have to worry about anyone?" I replied "I think we've had some of those days. And we've probably messed up some of those days. We are being tried, proven, tested, and more. We have a legacy to build. Yes, there will come a time (I think) where we can rest."

Once there, then what? What happened after David killed Goliath. What happened with Joseph after the famine had passed. What happened with Elijah and Elisha. We have bits and pieces of their full story. One day we will get to hear their whole stories. Until then (while I'm still here on this earth), I notice people's struggles (finances, homelessness, hopelessness, depression, hunger, and so on) within the natural and the spiritual realm.

Many don't know how to figure out the solution. They don't know where to turn or how to get out of the pit they've landed in. It saddens and upsets me. Many live paycheck to paycheck - just one issue or problem from financial ruin. Many don't have a clue how to walk a journey of faith. Many can't take their attention off the natural situation and turn to see what Holy Spirit is doing in the spiritual realm.

Many, too many, have very <u>real</u> natural problems that are extremely urgent and even deadly. The government doesn't have answers. A few churches (groups) help some, but mostly they care for their closest-knit flock. It is alarming to think of how the world's systems are setting the stage for the Antichrist. Many are being set up to be duped into following his agenda.

For now, I may not impact the 'many.' I may only impact a few (those closest to me). However, they can turn and impact others. A ripple effect begins and a legacy is built. My life here in this realm is just for a moment, but what I instill in others will last much longer. I am beginning to see that 'things' or material wealth is not important at all - except to be used as tools to help others experience Yahweh's Present Kingdom now.

Yahweh loves us beyond what we can even imagine. We are His most precious treasure. How do we cooperate in His process? How do we help the lost, broken, widows, orphans, sick, hungry, and hopeless? What did Jesus do? He did what He saw the Father doing. He loved, healed, cast out demons, raised the dead (naturally and spiritually dead), fed, taught... He spent time alone with the Father and prayed. He walked on water and turned water into wine. He commanded (used) His authority properly and in order. He told Peter to walk on the water and Peter walked on the Word of Jesus. Jesus rescued, died, redeemed, and rose again. He gave of Himself - laid His life down- for us all. He wept, sweat blood, and then actually shed His blood. He said we could do all that He did and even greater. Why aren't we doing this? We need to stop seeing ourselves as a group of weird misfit toys. We are unique because we can do what Jesus did.

My dream is not about me or just my small village. It's about the community, then the town, then the city, then the county and beyond. It's about teaching others to fish, to stretch, to go beyond what is humanly possible; because it's only with Yahweh that we can do greater things. I envision ways to help others to help themselves and each other. As I imagine the possibilities, Daddy asks "isn't that what you've done in building the village of helpers for Lindsey?" Wait, what? I've reached out to people to help Lindsey, and they were blessed in giving her assistance in her greatest time of trouble. Some might have forgotten what a blessing it is to give. Others may have known this secret all along.

Why is it that when you ride on a dream and experience an amazing thing, that you somehow come crashing down? Fear always tries to set in. It somehow looms over an uncertain future. My soul tries to fight the faith process. Oh dear. I don't want to stumble around and sleep-walk through life! The soul wants answers, but the mind has none. The soul wants a way around the circumstance, the mind tries to find one. I feel quite dense as I struggle with what I am to learn. I have no answers and no understanding. I don't want to tumble down into the valley. I want to run into what Yahweh has for me like David ran into the valley of Elah!

Haven't I learned that Yahweh holds my future in His hands. He is with me through everything. Sometimes I am afraid. I wonder what else I might have to walk through. Whew, I don't like this feeling! I don't hold onto it, I allow it to flow out of me onto Jesus. I really don't want to walk through even harder times to break this trait (or whatever it is). I want a simpler, less challenging life. I don't want to deal with cares, concerns, or burdens that try to weigh me down!! Yahweh does not condemn me. His heart is filled with loving kindness for me.

A picture pops into my mind - again one of that fateful night in the sea of Galilee during that massive storm that scared seasoned sailors. Jesus was not troubled. What did He see that was different from what the disciples saw? Jesus was in peace, they were not. The boat didn't keep the disciples safe, Jesus did! Jesus saw beyond the natural realm into the spiritual realm. He saw the

Father Who does not condemn us. He saw life, joy, and peace. What if we can change <u>our</u> beliefs about what we see? Through faith, we can see as Jesus sees. His question to me (and others) – "why are you afraid, oh you of little faith?" No matter what storm comes, I need not fear as He gives me authority over the storm. What a journey this has been!

JESUS CARRIES US

How does one share (write or tell) their deepest or hardest emotions? Some days are gentle and quiet, other days busy and hard. I think of Nick often as I spend time with Lindsey and the kiddos or even sometimes like this morning when I am still alone and not quite awake. I still can't believe that he is gone. What is Heaven's realm really like? Are there any regrets there? Can Nick see his children in this realm as they laugh, play, cry or argue? What of the two littles that went before him - does Nick play and laugh with them? I have too many unanswered questions. There are times when I walk with Jesus and other times when He has had to carry me.

A few weeks before Nick died, Paul (Lindsey's dad) was in my dream. It was amazing to see him. He looked the way he did when he was in his 30's. But the most amazing thing was all the "junk" - the illness he battled, the sorrow, the burdens - all the "negative" stuff were no longer in him or around him. He was genuinely happy - full of joy and peace. These positive feelings were literally tangible as I talked with him. It was as if I could reach out and touch the emotions. They poured out of Paul, surrounded him and spilled out into the atmosphere. The refreshing feelings touched and filled me. I was incredibly happy for him.

I believe the same wonderfulness holds true for Nick and any others that have moved on. They only experience the 'good', lovely, positive, and wonderful. The "junk" is left behind - here in this realm. It is unfortunate that we, who are here, still have to deal with the junk. I wish it were easier to let go of, here and now. Maybe we can learn to release some of it. Maybe that is what Yahweh really wants us to be able to do.

Soon another blessing will enter this world as Lindsey's and Nick's newest baby is born. Time will spin and whirl, and I don't quite know how to prepare myself for it. I have moments of sheer panic when I think any further ahead than today. Thankfully she and I don't have to walk this path alone. The small village of loving people have donated time, food, meals, and gifts. They have been such a blessing to Lindsey and our family. They've made it a little easier to walk through this incredibly difficult season. Still, I admit for the last week or more, I have stepped into a troublesome space. I've worried and questioned - how are we going to do this? I stumbled as I began to doubt my ability to take another step or do another task.

The days seem exceedingly long and hard, but I keep moving, trying to be a helper to Lindsey. Terry's been working hard, long hours at his job and not been able to help as much. I look forward sometimes to the end of the day. This is when I am able to relax and recuperate.

"Lord, I know You know all things. You do not forget Your promises. I ask again for the financial promise You have given me to manifest very soon. You know me, Lord, and You have given me a generous heart. You know of the great needs all around me. Let Your will be done, here on earth as it is in Heaven!!"

Once again 'noodle stick' prayers have come to my mind. When our hearts are not in alignment with Yahweh, we will doubt Him and His willingness and ability to answer our prayers. Recently I talked with "Brian." He questioned why God allowed His mom to suffer, especially at the end of her life. He felt 'bad' about his questions. I'm not sure if he realized that he had unbelief. But if he did, he didn't want to reveal that. Brian wasn't sure of the repercussions of questioning Yahweh. He was worried that somehow his questions would be met with Yahweh's anger. Where in the 'world' do we get these ideas (literally - as these ideas are not from or in Heaven).

For far too long, humans have misrepresented Yahweh and His love - we have missed the mark! Why does suffering happen? Why aren't people healed? When we pray, are we praying 'noodle stick' prayers? We ask Yahweh to heal someone, does He, in turn, ask us - "why are you asking Me to do something that I have given you the authority and the ability to do?" Jesus clearly said we can do His works and greater. He clearly gave us His authority. We have the right to exercise Holy Spirit's power. But we must remember whatever we can do is by Jesus' power and might, not ours. Let us stay humble and realize alone we can do nothing.

So... what happens when someone is damaged, hurt, or broken and they are not connected to Yahweh. Will Yahweh answer their prayers? I believe so, but I think healing begins inside the hurt individual first. As they are healed (mentally, emotionally, and spiritually), they can begin to utilize the gifts and fruit of Holy Spirit to help others. I wonder what is easier – to be healed physically or for the soul and spirit to be healed.

Seriously... can you imagine if all the people who claim to believe in Jesus actually DID what He did and lived their lives as He taught!? What if we accomplished the works of Jesus - lay our lives down in full submission to the will of the Father, heal, love, and walk rightly in His authority. When will we all realize that Christ lives His story through us - John 14:9-11,20. We aren't false imitators - we are Christians - like Christ!

My answer to Brian's question is simple - I believe that the Lord was with Brian's mother. He experienced all his mother experienced. Yahweh sent others to help her, yet maybe they were only able to do a certain amount because of their lack of faith and understanding. Maybe some of them failed at their task. Maybe they did all they could. Still, during her sojourn through the trials and sickness, I truly believe that Jesus carried her. He did not fail her. I believe she is no longer suffering. Her time here in this world is but a distant memory for her.

Jesus will carry you too - whoever you are, whatever you have done, wherever you go, He is there waiting for you to reach out to Him. He adores you so much that He died and rose again - for you.

GRACE

It's odd that yesterday, all afternoon, and into early evening I felt anxious, as though something was wrong or going to happen. I felt over sensitized and tired of the troubles. I asked Holy Spirit to give me more insight and revelation. I took a deep breath and released the worry and anxiety. It didn't take long for me to discover what I was sensing. I didn't know it yet, but I was getting ready to run into another valley and face another giant.

Later that same evening I had a scary call from Lindsey. K had eaten something with dairy in it, and the Benadryl had disappeared. I made a mad dash to the store and then to her home. What a harrowing journey full of heart racing minutes!! I prayed silently when K wouldn't (at first) take the medicine. He only had a few hives; therefore, Lindsey didn't have to give him an epinephrine injection or rush him to the hospital. For that, I'm incredibly grateful. Still, I cried all the way home. And I mean allllll the way home. I was venting: angry and afraid.

Yes, I trust Yahweh so why was I upset and bawling like a baby? My daughter handled the situation with incredible grace. Still, there were tears from her and me; there were scary and hard moments. Lindsey had to go through that terrifying event without Nick. He would have handled the situation calmly and professionally. That's part of who he was. We had confidence that Nick would know what to do in any medical emergency.

When I drove home (and I had to leave Lindsey with her wee

ones), I was angry that Nick is no longer here. He is no longer someone we can count on. I was afraid because I am not trained or very well prepared for emergency situations. Yes, I know fear is in opposition to faith. I don't like stepping out of faith into fear. Thankfully I don't stay long in that fearful place. I used to live there, in that fearful realm. I've learned I don't have to do that, I can choose to walk back into faith. Yes, there is room for a healthy kind of fear. That kind of fear alerts you to real and present danger. It is the kind that raises adrenaline, enabling one to do things beyond normal human strength.

Once I arrived back home, I thought of how Nick struggled while he walked this earth. I'm thankful he struggles no more. I miss him. I miss his competence in emergencies. I miss his wit. I miss the times that love filled his eyes when he looked at Lindsey or their little ones. Yes, we must keep walking in this journey. I don't like the grief that still tries to overwhelm me sometimes. Love and grace make it possible and other people make the journey easier.

Grace is defined as: graciousness (as gratifying), of manner or act (abstract or concrete; literal, figurative or spiritual; especially the divine influence upon the heart, and its reflection in the life; including gratitude):—acceptable, benefit, favour, gift, grace(-ious), joy, liberality, pleasure, thank(-s, -worthy). [1]

Grace (for me) means Yahweh gives all we need to accomplish whatever is set before us. Grace is the ability to walk through each valley, fight & kill the giants, calm the storms, conquer new territory, etcetera. Grace is the peace, rest, or trust that Yahweh will be there with us. Couldn't we all use a little grace?

NOTE

[1] G5485 - charis - Strong's Greek Lexicon (KJV). Retrieved from https://www.blueletterbible.org//lang/Lexicon/Lexicon.cfm?Strongs=G5485&t=KJV

NEW LIFE

I got the call around 4:00 a.m. - Lindsey was in labor and off I went to watch the other kiddos. Her newest son was born around 9 a.m. on November 4, 2016. Nick's mom got to stand where Nick should have been. She was with Lindsey in the delivery room the whole time. Later that day, I was able to hold my fifth grandchild. I fell in love all over again. It's amazing how love can expand and fill your chest. Somehow your heart makes room for more. There's always more room for love. I stand in awe at how Yahweh has brought such beauty out of ashes. I'm amazed how even in the deepest valley, one can find joy, peace, and love. Wow, such amazing love. I am a blessed woman.

I remember when I gave birth to Lindsey and Angelica and how love multiplied. I remember they were the reason I got up each time I was knocked down. I fought and kept going because of that multiplied love. I learned the great power of love will keep your head above the water even if you're lost in a sea of storms.

Multiple years later my first granddaughter graced us with her arrival. Love multiplied. Then with the arrival of each new grandchild love multiplied again and again. I truly treasure the lovely moments. What great reasons to take the next step.

Yet, I am sad that Nick isn't here to enjoy the grand love of his and Lindsey's children. Maybe he is in some ways. Maybe because love resonates, it can crisscross between the realms. Maybe love knows no boundaries. Many have stepped in to shower the little ones with love. They soak it in like little flowers soak in the rain.

During the blessing of new birth, the enemy tries to step in and stir up trouble. I want to cry and beat the air with my fists out of my frustration. A skirmish with Terry left me hurt and angry. I won't give complete details as this is not important. What is important is that we work through each and every issue. We must realize we are fighting an unseen enemy and not each other. We must realize that our words have creative power. Harsh or negative words can create a wall of sorts between two people. Physical walls can be climbed, walked around, or even walked through once an opening is made.

How does one get around spiritual walls? It's especially hard when the other person has created the wall. How do you get around the emotions hard words create? I suppose the first step is you must <u>want</u> to conquer the wall. You can't force yourself, as this will only cause you to dig in your heels and you'll rebel. Geez, how my contrary flesh wanted to hang onto the offense, keep the wall up, and add more bricks and mortar to the wall. Before I could do so, Terry took a 'time out.' If he had pushed up against the wall or tried to tear it down, I'm sure I could have found some nasty bricks to add to the mix. My spirit doesn't like this whole mess. My soul argues as I didn't cause this. My spirit knows we need to create anew - tear down the wall, make a way. This battle sucks; it's very hard. It rages inside. Terry didn't make much of an attempt to be a wall destroyer. I need help taking this wall down. I need kind and gentle words of assurance. Can't Holy Spirit reach into Terry's spirit and give him another wake-up call.

The Lord reminds me that I am a change agent and He has given me much grace. He has forgiven me for much more than this simple offense. I peer into the spiritual realm and closely inspect the wall that Terry's words built. Why doesn't Terry see it? After all, he built the darn wall, and it's right there in between us! Part of my soul wants to take off a brick and hit him with it. Not only is this line of thinking not helpful, it would cause more damage, and it really isn't who I am or how I act.

Yahweh will work within us – to help us become more like Jesus. I have laid my life down (it really is <u>His life</u> I live not mine). Jesus didn't wait for anyone to feel remorse before He literally laid His life down on that cross. He did what He came to do in full obedience to the Father's will. He didn't deserve the things done to Him. He never sinned, rebelled, threw bricks, or built walls. He simply forgave. He made the choice to do what was right and what we really needed. He never questioned, "how is this fair?" Fairness would have kept Him in the Heavenly realm.

Why do humans hurt one another? Maybe it's because they don't realize they are made in the image and likeness of Yahweh. We aren't created to be selfish or self-seeking. I have to walk this faith journey out and lay down my perception of 'being right' or what's fair. The stress and conflict cause very real physical symptoms in my body. I don't like this process!!!

It took some time, but Terry and I were able to disassemble that brick wall. Looking back, it wasn't a very big wall. I hope we stop building walls altogether. Maybe we can discover a new way, a new life...

LAST CALL

On the 6th of November, we celebrated Nick's life in the church where he and Lindsey were married. It was hard to sit in that seat and wait for the service to begin. I could not contain my tears as I looked around the church and scenes from Lindsey's and Nick's wedding day played over and over in my mind. I looked down the long aisle that Paul struggled to walk down. He was determined to use a cane, not a walker. He fought hard to walk at all after his accident. He was very proud and couldn't wait to surprise Lindsey by how far he had come.

I remember how happy Nick and Lindsey were on that wonderful day. I remember the ceremony that joined them as one. That entire wedding party was there today, everyone but Nick. Could he see us? Did he take note of the many who came because they love him? Was Paul able to see the day's events? I have too many questions with no answers.

Throughout the service, I kept a watchful eye on Lindsey. I was very concerned for her. She seemed determined not to show the physical pain from having the baby via caesarian section **or** the emotional pain from the loss of Nick. I knew it, I could feel it. Yes, it was hard to be there, but I'm glad I was there for her.

Before Lindsey sat down, she turned toward me and signed 'I love you' while she patted her chest.

No-one knows how hard it was to remain in my seat and not run to her, especially when her tears hit me like a wave.

Certain moments within the service literally took my breath away, and I sobbed as quietly as I could. Some of Nick's friends spoke and I liked hearing how much they loved him. The Reverend also spoke highly of Nick; clearly, his heart was touched as well. Lindsey shared her heart – a tribute to Nick and a letter written to their new baby boy.

Then the paramedic team performed the last call. I'd never experienced that before. What an honor they bestowed upon Nick. I can't recall the exact words the paramedic Manager spoke, but I know I will never forget Nick's name being called over the radio for the last time. They honored him again by announcing his number was officially retired; it can never be used again. I forgot how to breathe when Lindsey was given a folded flag. She might keep it beside the one given to her at her father's funeral only six months ago, in May.

After the service, everyone moved downstairs for a short time to eat and share memories of Nick. I sat at a table, feeling the effects of stress and too little sleep. I felt "off" - almost other worldly. Maybe I was walking in the spiritual realm. Maybe my blood sugar was dropping. Maybe as a burden bearer, I felt too much of the grief.

I finally sat down, and I suddenly noticed a man who looked like Elvis. An even stranger feeling came over me. For me, Elvis is a sign from Yahweh - He used an Elvis wannabe to prove I am here on (and for a) purpose. I wonder what this Elvis sighting meant...

Lindsey had to return to the hospital (as she wasn't discharged, she only had a day pass). I cannot imagine how incredibly difficult that day was for her.

After the service, Terry and I went to see the kiddos. They were playing in the leaves, laughing, running, oh my.... such beauty out of the ashes!

I honestly believe that only love and grace helped Lindsey (well all of us) through that entire day. Love and grace will have to continue to help us all.

When Lindsey and her new baby, J, come home from the hospital. I'll be there. Others will join in at times to help carry the load while Lindsey heals. We welcomed and appreciated every prayer, meal, and donation. Everyone was & continues to be incredibly generous. It's a blessing to know that Lindsey and her little ones are loved. And while she gets blessed, those who help her will be blessed as well. It'll be a blessing to continue helping with the kiddos. It'll be a blessing to love and snuggle them. It'll be a blessing to hold J and breathe in that new baby smell.

The days flew by and before we knew it, Lindsey and her new baby boy came home from the hospital on the 8th of November. I knew it would be overwhelming for her. What a journey. J is very precious! M and K fell in love the minute they saw him. It was sweet - bittersweet. I wish that Nick could have been there. Yes, to help but also to see all the beauty that Yahweh has brought out of these ashes. Yahweh gives us oil of joy out (from within) the mourning and a garment of praise instead of a spirit of despair.

Even though I was frustrated with the health of my frail body, I looked to Daddy. I cried out for His ever Present help and I continued to praise Him.

It was weird (in a sense) that the whole country was focused on the election at this point in time. Yes, the election was important. Yes, I voted (stood in an hour-long line, dead tired, stomach hurting, and feet burning). If you wonder why I bothered ... my vote counts. Women fought for the right to vote. I can't imagine what they went through. Still, I didn't have the time or energy to worry or wonder who the next U.S. President would be. I was just trying to take the next step in front of me. I will continue to do that, as long as the Lord leads.

CHARACTER AND INTEGRITY

It's been a little over a month since Nick left earth and entered Heaven's realm. I've been trying to help Lindsey as much as I can. I am tired and in physical and emotional pain. I want more, so much more - for my children and for me. Natural circumstances too often garner my attention! I've been reading a new book this evening, and it (like many others before it) applies to what I am experiencing right here, right now. I am glad that Yahweh is still making connections. One dot connecting another dot forms a piece of the picture in my mind's eye. Every dot (instance) carries meaning and purpose. They are multi-layered, multicolored, and multifaceted. It's amazing that I can 'see' these connections and how Yahweh has worked them out. There was a time I wouldn't have been able to see them at all. I would love to be able to draw or paint what I see. My words will have to suffice.

I know that many times, I became fixated on accomplishing the dream Yahweh's given me. He's not concerned about that - He's more interested in me and my becoming all He has created me to be. Maybe I can't have the full realization of the dream until I literally become what He designed. I ask Yahweh to sanctify my motives. I really am not worried about getting credit or even being noticed. I want to remain humble. I want to walk in Yahweh's integrity and character. I should be careful what I ask for.

I went to the store and got two plates with dividers in them along with some other items. The plates were stuck together, and I thought the cashier only rang up one of them. I felt prompted to ask her, but I didn't because I was exhausted. I left the store and got into my car. The entire time, an argument was going on inside of me. It truly bothered me to think I may have left the store and may have only paid for one of the plates. Finally, I grabbed the receipt and knew if I didn't pay for two, I'd have to go back into that store. Thankfully both plates were on the receipt. Whew! I could have saved myself an argument had I just spoke up in the store. But, I 'needed' to walk through this lesson.

To some, this may seem a small thing. For me, it carried a lot of 'weight' in the spirit. This was a test of integrity. It serves to grow, mold, and change me so that I may have the same character as Jesus does. I came close to missing the mark over two silly plates.

I think of various "famous" Christian pastors or teachers. I wonder why they don't often share their mistakes or failures? Certainly, everyone has them. When people don't share them, it's as if a big part of the picture is missing. Are pastors or teachers being fully authentic if they don't share the test along with the testimony? Am I somehow missing something because I make mistakes and fail. Maybe the speakers don't want to be transparent because they think the audience won't listen to them. However, when people can see our struggles, they can relate more to us. We don't have to model ourselves after any specific leader today.

It's important for me to write: when I am talking about character and integrity, I am not saying we must behave perfectly. We cannot do this as only Jesus is perfect. I just think we should be open about our experiences. We don't have to fit a certain mold and we can admit our flaws or mistakes. We are forgiven, and we can be utilized by Yahweh! My hope is to encourage you with some interesting tidbits about some of the famous biblical greats.

Adam disobeyed Yahweh and shifted blame. Eve was deceived. Moses stuttered and was short tempered. Miriam and Aaron gossiped about Moses. Aaron also formed an idol out of gold for the Israelites to worship. Abraham and Sarah were old when they finally had a child. But before that, Abraham (per Sarah's insistence) got Sarah's maid pregnant.

Rebekah was manipulative. Noah got drunk and lay naked in his tent. Gideon doubted and thought he didn't have any value. David didn't fit into the lent armor. He had an affair and had the woman's husband killed. He was troubled and battled deep despair.

Elijah was discouraged, weary, and full of fear. Jonah was angry and ran away. Job suffered great loss and struggled deeply. Jeremiah was lonely, defeated, and insecure. Hosea's wife was a prostitute. Jacob was a liar.

Martha was overly worried. Peter, James & John slept while Jesus prayed. Peter was afraid and denied Jesus three times. Everyone deserted Jesus when He was crucified. Timothy doubted. Mark deserted Paul and Barnabas. Paul and Barnabas had a strong disagreement and ended up going separate ways.

Each of these had flaws, but each person serves a purpose. The key is not to get stuck in the flaws, instead simply flow in your purpose.

VISION

I wrote the following while I sat in my car at the river....

I often feel disappointed as I want to move forward in this faith journey. I need to keep the vision for the promise Yahweh gave me. I don't know what lies ahead, but I must move anyway. I don't want to settle for scraps or leftovers, I want all that Yahweh has for me. But lately, it seems I've reached the end of my rope (of myself). I don't seem to have any strength left. My legs hurt, and my stomach/gut has been iffy for days now. I'm ill, frustrated, and tired. I physically can't take another step. I wouldn't even know where to place my foot. Depression lurks around like a cat preparing to pounce a mouse. I struggle to move, and I am overwhelmed, to say the least. My spirit continues to fight to remain. My soul wearies of the battle. I am done, just done.   There is none who can help me but Yahweh. If He doesn't, then I will sink deeper into this pit of depression and illness. I want out, but it's like I'm in a mud hole with slippery sides and I can't get hold of anything to pull myself out. One thing after another crops up to cause more concerns to rain down upon me in this mud pit. I try to remember that others have it much worse. Well that doesn't help at all! I try to remember that this natural world is temporary. Nope, still not helping. I can't help but see my offerings as meager and don't know if the help I do provide is enough.

I purposefully take my mind off how I feel. I turn my attention to the sights around me. How I love the beauty and simplicity of this place!! I enjoy the 'stillness' in Yahweh's Presence. The river has light ripples across it. I can't help but think of the ripple effect... One person touches another person's life and that person helps another, on and on it goes. Even the smallest gesture can have an impact (good or bad). Why don't more people seek to do good? While some are self-seeking and selfish, others give in abundance. Has it always been this way? Such a mixture of those who freely give and those who do not. Certainly, Jesus gave freely – is that why Jesus stood out from the crowd? When Holy Spirit searches the spirit and soul of someone, isn't He looking for the signs of Jesus' life?

The seasons change, and as each one arrives, I wonder what new things it will bring. When time is freed up (where I am not helping Lindsey as much), what shall I do then? What adventures will Holy Spirit take me into? What vision can I focus on now? To help me direct my focus, I created vision boards to help me to remember what Yahweh has done. Basically, I bought two poster boards to which I glued pictures, words, and scripture verses. The first board is designed to remind me of what Yahweh has already accomplished. I have a picture or two for each of the stories in my first book. The second board is meant to help me to look forward to what Yahweh will do. For example, I have pictures of a large house with a big porch where people could meet, campgrounds, gold, an RV convoy, and so on.

I suppose I can also write the vision the Lord has given me. I have written some notes, but it's not detailed. I really don't what I should write. I also know that the vision will not manifest until it's appointed time.

I shared my vision board ideas with Rob Stoppard. Then I told him about the Elvis wannabe who showed up at Nick's memorial service. I also mentioned how someone I knew from long ago had recently posted (on Facebook) a video with Elvis singing. I told him I realized that Rae of Hope isn't just for me. Then I asked Rob what he thought these Elvis sightings meant. Rob wrote: "Elvis had a lasting impact, influence, and legacy. He left a mark on the world that people still talk about today. His style is unique and has been duplicated/replicated many times. The vision you carry is designed to touch generations alive today and many that will follow. Your vision can be replicated anywhere on the earth. Elvis showing up is an affirmation of something very big. So, do not grow wear in the 'bigness' but look for the next steps from Holy Spirit."

The following morning after reading Rob's email, I started thinking about the Israelites again. The Israelites complained a lot while they were in the wilderness. Perhaps they didn't truly trust Yahweh and they didn't know Him as a good Father. Maybe Yahweh was trying to instill His character and integrity in them. Their vision was clouded, even though Yahweh was clearly within their sight. Were they frustrated or disappointed most of the time? Did they somehow lose the vision for the promise Yahweh had given them?

What I am feeling and experiencing doesn't match the huge vision deep inside of me. I can't find any way to accomplish it – I know good and well that only Yahweh can make the vision happen. I cry out: Yahweh!!! I need rest and encouragement. All I know to do is cling to Jesus in faith. He will bring His vision for my life to fruition. I trust Yahweh.

BUGGED

I do not understand why strange things happen to me. Maybe it's to teach me something. Maybe it's to make me pay attention. Well, this is what had me bugged -- I found ONE bed bug on my chair in Terry's house. It set me off in quite the tizzy. Anyone who knows me knows that I detest creepy crawly things. Not long after Terry and I were married, his house was invaded by ants. I thought they were bad – but this darn bed bug was 100 times worse. That tiny creature brought up some harboring wounds and old baggage. It is so weird how little things will trigger you and cause a whole host of issues. That stupid bug made me look at my circumstances and the choices which have kept me in a place I DO NOT want to be. The picture I saw wasn't pretty. I allowed my peace, joy, and contentment to be taken. Depression lurked around me like some sulking giant. It tried to instill hopelessness. I promptly ignored the feelings instead of venting or dealing with them.

What do people do when they feel they have lost all hope and direction? Some might deal with the issue or extinquish the fire. Others allow the fire burn all around them. I <u>had</u> to deal with the bed bug, even if I didn't want to deal with the feelings. I ran every possible piece of clothing through the hottest setting on the dryer. I sprayed down every possible surface with 90% isopropyl alcohol. I ended up with the worst headache, and my mind battled with sadness. I'd had enough and went to the river. I couldn't pretend that all was well within my world. I wouldn't know how. The river was covered with snow and ice yet the current still flowed underneath. It slowly moved the snow/ice rafts, taking the seagulls that landed there for a ride. Stupid birds, why don't they fly away to someplace warmer, a better climate? Can't they find a better place to be? What about me - why don't I fly away to some better place...

I sat by the riverside for some time as I watched the birds and pondered my situation. The bed bug situation was beyond my comprehension. I have no idea where it came from. I was worried the house was overrun with the creepy critters. I needed to take a stand. So, I decided I would refuse to sleep in the house until I was assured there were no more of the creepy critters. I wasn't sure where I'd go – I certainly didn't want to risk the bugs following me to another place.

I ended up sleeping alone in my travel trailer. Terry made a clear choice to ignore me and the entire issue. He would probably say he didn't know what to do or that he didn't want to make matters worse. So, he did nothing. I felt abandoned. I was left alone to figure things out on my own. Of course, I did not want empty placating words spilling out of Terry into my tender ears. I wanted tangible actions to move forward into the life I am designed to walk.

What can I do, what must I do. I suppose I was forced to deal with what was right in front of me. I had an exterminator investigate and fumigate Terry's house. Interestingly, he could find no other bed bugs. I don't know what happened. Hopefully, over time I will glean more lessons from that one single bug.

Not long after the bed bug issue was finalized. I went to an evening worship service. I was told - - 'You have walls up and the Lord is going to take them down. There was a gate, but He has the key and has unlocked it. A huge wave is coming, a tsunami; but don't be afraid, it is of God. He is your anchor, cling to Him.' I didn't ask for this message. I didn't say anything to the person who spoke that message to me. But I did wrestle with for a few days. At least the bed bugs weren't mentioned or seen again.

The following Sunday morning, after the worship service, I told the Pastor a little bit about my struggles, and he prayed. I told him of the message and my concerns. He told me that the best part of that message is that God is my anchor through it all. And whatever the enemy means to destroy, God will turn it all around. Because I've been through so much, there are even greater things coming. God will have huge things for me.

A few weeks flew by in which I managed to remain at Terry's house. We managed to talk through the reasons I felt bugged. And it amazes me that even though I may not have behaved properly, the Lord knew my heart, and He still used me to speak a few words on a Sunday morning church service. I should write things down before I get up to speak because I tend to get very nervous. I didn't say it quite right, but this is the message: "the Lord would say I am blowing a fresh wind, that wind is My Spirit. The wind will blow over the dry bones bringing them to life. Everyone matters."

I don't understand the meaning behind: the message of the bed bug, the message of the walls, gate and wave, and the message of a fresh wind blowing over dry bones. I am sure there is some connection that I don't quite see yet. There are no coincidences.

THANKSGIVING

Even though there was a chill in the air, I spent a few stolen moments at the river. I love the beauty and simplicity of that place. A few people were out in boats and one man was fishing. Are there any fish to catch in that cold water? How do they withstand the chill?

I can't help but wonder – what changes are coming, what will the Christmas season bring. How and when should I let go and let Lindsey fully manage her life without much of my help. It's hard to let go but I must. What will I do when she doesn't need me so much. I just have to trust the Lord to show me what to do.

Today is Thanksgiving and of course, my mind reviews past Thanksgivings. They were not a big deal for me. Angelica likes this holiday; I think because it's close to her birthday. Lindsey has always liked watching the parades on TV. For me, it seems like all you do is a lot of work to prepare a huge meal. After filling my belly with all that food, I just want to take a nap. Maybe the best part is having leftover turkey for days, which means less time in the kitchen.

This year I have dedicated some time to make Thanksgiving dinner at Lindsey's. This is their first holiday without Nick. There will be ashes. I hope we also see the beauty. The little ones are good eaters and they always seem thankful for the food they eat.

I wonder if today will just be another ordinary day for the wee ones. Will they notice the place Nick left behind. Does Heaven celebrate this day or is every day a celebration there. Time and space aren't the same there as it is here. In Heaven, everyone and everything celebrates Yahweh.

Can those in Heaven see us here on earth? Do they realize how much they are missed? Even though I am thankful for all Yahweh has done, I still feel melancholy. It's not the deep feelings of grief, just a prevailing sadness. I won't dwell on it, yet I won't try to hide it either. Instead, I think of the meaning of this holiday – thankfulness. I also think about the love we all share.

I read 1 Corinthians 13 - the love chapter. Verses 4-7 describe love - Yahweh is pure love, that is Who He is. I looked closer at verse three... If I gave <u>everything</u> I have to the poor and even sacrificed my body, I could boast about what I'd done, but if I didn't <u>love</u> others, I would have <u>gained</u> nothing. Without love, life isn't worth living. If people aren't experiencing love, how do they even function? Yahweh pours out His love freely in abundance to us. Now that is something to be thankful for! Actually, we should be thankful for all Yahweh offers to us.

In my last book, I wrote about the prodigal son, but I missed a very important point. The story is found in Luke 15:11-32. The younger son squandered his inheritance while the older son remained at home. The father allowed the younger son to leave and did not go out after him. He waited for that son to come home. When he finally did come home, the older son was offended and refused to go in to the celebration that the father held for the younger son.

Here is what I missed before - the father went out after the older son and pleaded with him (see verse 28). Then the father said, "My son, you are always with me, and all that I have is yours" (Luke 15:31 NKJV). At any point in time, the older son could have had a celebration. Why didn't he? The older son was never lost - he remained with the father.

This is odd, but for some reason, I didn't picture the father being as happy, giving, or loving toward the older son. However, now I see something new. While the younger son gallivanted around – that entire time - the older son was <u>home</u> with the father. He was being loved and blessed. And when the older son walked away (albeit very briefly), the father followed him and reassured him.

I wonder which part I have played – which 'son' am I most like. Wasn't I like the son who ran away, squandered his life and eventually returned to the Father. Haven't I also been like the older son. Don't we all, at times, forget who we are and what we have access to?

Our Heavenly Father <u>will</u> happily seek out those who are lost. He will go after anyone who walks away (whether it's a long period or a short time). The Father celebrates each one of us. Every single one of us is valuable to Yahweh. He doesn't grow angry with us and He doesn't chastise us when we run away from Him. He doesn't grow tired of us if we throw a pity party. He doesn't get upset with us if we become offended or jealous. He will wait for us or even come after us. Therefore, can't we see that every day is Thanksgiving for Him because every day is an opportunity to welcome someone back to Himself!

PIGEON FORGE

Christmas day, after I got to see my grandchildren open their gifts, Terry and I headed off for a short vacation to Pigeon Forge Tennessee. A friend had posted (on Facebook) about the Gatlinburg fire and requested any help anyone could give. I gathered up some non-perishable food to take down. We'd decided to spend our vacation money in an area that desperately needed the help.

We stopped in Roanoke Virginia to spend the night. We both were tired and fell asleep quickly. I woke up around 2:00 a.m. The left side of my face was itchy, red, and puffy with hives. My throat was scratchy, and it was slowly getting worse. I woke up Terry, and he took me to the closest hospital, where the Doctor pumped me full of antihistamine and steroids. Why did that event happen? I don't know the purpose or reason. I just know it was really scary. I could have freaked out and insisted on returning home. Terry recognized this fact and said, "in the past, you would have wanted to go home." Had we returned, we would have missed out on all that the Lord had for us. Was it an attack? Maybe, but Yahweh turns all things to the good.

After we left the hospital, we headed off to Pigeon Forge and the hotel that I had booked through an online agency. Well, I'll never do that again! The hotel room was filthy, so we quickly left. We found a much nicer hotel not too far away from the first.

The Titanic museum was the first adventure on our vacation. It took us three and a half hours to experience it all. That's probably because we took our time and we read most of the information posted. In one of the rooms, we discovered information on Molly Brown. Debbie Reynolds starred in the movie based on her life. Before we had left the hotel, the news reported Debbie Reynolds had just passed away.

The musicians played music till the Titanic sunk. The museum used the catch phrase "when the music stopped, the legend began." Terry said if he'd been on board he would have broken a door off its hinges, tied a rope, and made a raft. He would have fought to survive. I'm not sure what I would have done. I looked at each picture of those talented musicians - were they heroes? They didn't scurry about or help to load the passengers into life boats. They did WHAT they WERE. They played music, which has the power to calm the soul. Certainly, they must have known there was little else for them to do. Certainly, their gift (of music) helped the others.

I recall that many years ago, someone said that the United States and maybe the Church was like the Titanic. Back then, I wondered why the musicians just sat playing music, while the ship sunk. I had discounted the work the musicians did. Surely there were not indifferent! Surely, they were giving all of themselves to soothe or comfort the others. It goes to show that each one of us, operating in our calling and utilizing our gifts serve a very important role. Even if the offering is just a small comfort to a small group, it's still important. For instance, the small amount of food Terry and I donated to the town helped. That food was like the few 'fishes' and 'loaves.' Yahweh shall multiply.

Another adventure Terry and I went on was the Escape Game.

What a blast! We had to discover clues and figure them out to escape in 60 minutes or less. The six people in the game had to work as a team, and each one of us figured out at least one clue. The game gives you three free clues, but any additional hints or clues cost you time on the clock. There were three separate areas within the game. We had to find three pieces of fake gold. We used all our free clues and escaped before the 60 minutes were up.

On another day, we visited a store called the Pigeon Forge Gem Mine. I sifted through a dirt bucket to find rough gem stones. I found several but chose a sapphire and an amethyst to be cut and polished. It's interesting that Sapphire could symbolize Heaven. Sapphire is mentioned as a representation of one of the tribes in the high priests' breastplate - Exodus 28:17-20. It will decorate one of the foundations of the new Jerusalem - Revelation 21:19. Amethyst is also one of the precious stones in the breastplate of the high priest, and it'll also be in the foundation of the new Jerusalem.

On another day, Terry and I visited the Aquarium in Gatlinburg. It is wonderful, and we had such fun. It was sobering to discover that the Aquarium came very close to being destroyed by the fire. Every living creature in that place is dependent upon an entire complicated system to keep them healthy and alive. What (or should I say Who) held that fire at bay.

Our final adventure was when Terry and I celebrated my birthday by going to eat snow crab legs at an all you can eat buffet. And we ate all we could! It was very good. Originally, we'd intended on going to the restaurant later that evening. But Terry opted to leave a few hours sooner. We drove around a few minutes and even took a wrong turn. Once we arrived, we got seated right away. Our server, Lynn, was quiet but prompt and courteous.

After Terry and I stuffed ourselves, we got our coats on and prepared to leave. I felt Holy Spirit told me to speak to Lynn, but she'd already walked away. I told Him if He wants me to say something to her, He'd have to bring her back around - of course, He did. I love how He works! Basically, I said to her "you are going through a struggle, but the Lord is going to work it out." Oh my, the look on her face - full of surprise and amazement. I know she needed that simple word from the Lord and I am in awe of Yahweh's timing. He caused us to be there at that restaurant at that exact time so that she would be our waitress. Wow. I want to do that more! I ask Holy Spirit 'show up and show off in Lynn's life. Let her see You, to know You and to have real experiences of You, Yahweh. I know You love her. You ARE love. Thank You for the opportunity to speak into her heart.'

I am reminded of 'triangulation' - how Yahweh connects the dots; how He leaves us clues to discover Who He is and who we are, and to learn of our purpose. On the trip back home, Terry asked me "so what's up with the threes?" The first hotel (in Virginia) was on the third floor, but neither of us could remember the number (it would have started with the number three). We didn't stay at the dirty hotel, but I did find a quarter there. In the second hotel, our room number was 333 (in Tennessee). And for our final hotel stay back in Virginia, our room number was 303.

We stayed in three hotels for a total of 7 nights. Furthermore, Terry and I went to three major attractions. We were in the Titanic museum for three and a half hours. The Escape Game had several instances of the number three (or 3 x 2 = 6). Three has great significance in the Bible...

The number three appears 485 times in the KJV of the Bible. The number three is a picture of completeness (though to a lesser significant degree than 7). There are three divisions of time in the natural world: past, present, future. As I said before Yahweh, Jesus, Holy Spirit are Three but One. Jesus went 'missing' for 3 days when He was 12 - Luke 2:46. He was in His 30's when He began His ministry. His ministry lasted 3 years. Jesus prayed 3 times in Gethsemane. He was put on the cross at the third hour (9 a.m.) and died at the ninth hour (3 p.m.). Three hours of darkness covered the land while He suffered on the cross. He was dead 3 days, 3 nights.

I am amazed at the crazy amazing things Yahweh did during the vacation in Pigeon Forge and Gatlinburg. It greatly encouraged and refreshed Terry and me. I highly recommend this as a vacation destination. I hope all who go there will find fun, adventure, and even clues to Yahweh's activity in their lives!

ROOTS AND FRUITS

I began thinking about trees – specifically, I ponder the fruit and roots of the tree. I wondered, how are they connected. In the natural, the produce (fruit) is a direct result of the seed planted. This is also true in the spiritual realm. Let's take a deeper look at the spiritual roots deep inside each of us...

It's easy to look at how someone is behaving (noticing their 'fruit") and judge them or decide certain things about them. Most forget that deep inside, every soul is valuable to the Lord and His Kingdom.

Galatians chapter five contrasts the fruit of a sinful nature with the fruit of Holy Spirit. Most would agree the latter is a better option. We are born with a sinful nature, and if left alone we'd be lost. We do not have to remain in that lost state. We can allow Holy Spirit to guide our lives. We can obtain the great benefits of His fruit and His gifts. He can and will deal with the issues inside of us. I have allowed (and continuously allow) Him free access to every part of me. Is it easy, no. Every so often, something will happen (I'll be 'triggered') and part of me will try to revert to the old way or habit.

I can usually trace the incident back down through history to an old bad "root" which needs tended to. I'm fully dependent on Holy Spirit's work because a great deal of my memory (from infancy up to my early teenage years) is inaccessible to me.

Someday, I may need deeper exploration, but I leave the revelation up to Holy Spirit. In the meantime, I continually open myself up to Holy Spirit's work inside of me. I am able to stop, drop and roll... I **"stop"** and realize what I am experiencing and feeling. I ask – "okay where is this coming from?" Or "what is this feeling?" I then **"drop"** the issue/problem/feeling into the hands of Jesus. I ask Holy Spirit to dive deep into my spirit and soul and do whatever work is necessary. He knows what the root is, and He knows exactly what must be done. Then comes **"roll"** – I let Him take me through whatever process is necessary. Certainly, alone I can do nothing, but in Christ, I can do all things.

The process may involve facing an old mountain, being led around it and walking out from around it in a new and healthier way. Sometimes it's walking into the valley. Or it may be sitting by the brook of "Cherith" - resting and waiting upon Yahweh. Sometimes it's picking up the Sword and cutting the giant's head off. Sometimes it's facing the storm, keeping my eyes on Jesus, and then walking on the water. One day, I hope to help others discover their own unique abilities, talents, and gifts. I hope to let them learn how to "stop, drop, and roll.' I hope to help others see that their actions (fruit) are directly linked to the deep roots inside of them and to where they were planted (where they came from).

SEED AND SOIL

It is important to allow Holy Spirit to shine His light on the roots buried deep inside of us. I think we must also consider the soil in which the seed is planted. If a seed falls by the wayside, it won't even get the chance to form roots and grow. Seed sown on shallow soil will produce quick sprouts. But those plants will soon die without deep roots. Seed sown among thorns (worry, abuse, addiction, and even life's pleasures) soon die. However, seed sown in fertile (good, healthy, Christ centered) soil will produce a bountiful harvest.

Check out the Parable of the Farmer Scattering Seed (found in Matthew 13, Mark 4, Luke 8). Jesus explained the parable: Yahweh is the Farmer and the Word is the seed (sown by Yahweh often through us). The devil is the thief who steals the Word from people's hearts. Seed sown on rocky ground may be received with joy, but after being tested, the person falls away. Seed that lands among thorns will be choked and won't mature. Seed on good ground will produce a good crop

Let's say we are the tree (which has roots and produces fruit). We started as a 'seed.' Many are sown (planted) into harsh places. We have no control over where we are sown (i.e. which family or environment we are born into). No one knows another's full history (the soil or roots formed there). The process to heal, be repaired or restored is unique to the individual.

It could be that the entire tree will have to be uprooted, moved, and replanted into the good soil of Jesus. Maybe there is just one root that has to be torn out. What if the entire root system has to be reestablished!

I grew up on a farm, and each year my family had a huge garden. There was this one particular plant that we called something akin to the darn enemy. Weird, I know. It seemed that whole plant and its roots were long and prickly. If I wasn't careful, I'd get hooked or cut by that plant/root. Often, as I pulled up that irritating plant, the root would break off in the ground. It wasn't long before it would raise its ugly head. And as soon as that stupid plant would pop up out of the ground, the whole battle with the darn enemy would begin again.

When faced with that sort of experience (digging up our own roots), since we really don't know what we are doing, we might cause more damage to ourselves (and others). Some might even end up being hooked on something (addicted). We could end up feeling estranged from Yahweh and others. Alone, how can anyone deal with old roots of pain and wounds? For most, it'd be hard to imagine a better way. Try to picture someone who had been planted in good soil from the start! Imagine if that person's roots were fed the good food of love, acceptance, grace, mercy, and Christ-centered identity!

Alas, I cannot go back to before I was born. I cannot change the past. All I can do is allow Holy Spirit to continue His work inside of me. Maybe I will get uprooted at times. Maybe the "darn enemy" must be completed annihilated so I don't get hooked or cut or damaged (and so I don't do any of those things to others). Maybe old wounds must be reopened, cauterized and allowed to heal properly. I pray that many of the bad roots have been removed and good roots have begun to take hold. I pray much of the healing work has already taken place.

I know for certain that we are born into the time and space allotted by Yahweh. He knows all we will face. He will turn everything to the good – to benefit us as individuals and to benefit others we will meet along the way. Holy Spirit can reveal the old roots. His removal and healing methods are more effective than ours. Jesus prunes away the dead parts of the plants to allow the healthy parts to thrive. I don't really look forward to the process – digging up, rooting out, cauterizing, pruning, and so on. Yahweh, Your will be done in me as it is in Heaven.

NEW YEAR, NEW SEASON

It's a few days after New Years of 2017, and though it's cold, I am at the river. The quiet surrounds me – all except for the seagulls and a few ducks making their calls. I think of each of my grandchildren - each with their own personality and ways. I treasure them. I also think about the two deaths in our family. I thought the holiday season would be excruciating. However, it was gentle on us all.

Memories of Paul and Nick remain - that's all we have left of them here. Some days I can't believe they are gone. Other days it's almost as if they were never here to begin with. Their deaths make me realize how important it is to have a legacy - something that will last for generations. Many cultures share their history in stories to the younger generations. It's odd that I've not thought much about a legacy until this past year. Maybe it's just a rite of passage - when you reach a certain age, you realize you're not meant to remain here in this natural world and you want to leave something behind.

What can I build that will last for many generations? I pray I realize the value in what I am doing today. Material wealth is only important here, in this place. Too many people spend countless amounts of time, energy, and money on material things that don't last. Most believe only in the here and now; they are totally unaware of the greater promises of Yahweh.

For sure, Yahweh allows (and wants) us to enjoy this journey of life with Him. Yet, in the end, we are meant for more than this short lifespan. We are meant for a relationship with Him for an eternity.

I pray I continue to walk out this great story of Jesus, faith, and hope. I shall continue to look for instances where Holy Spirit is presently active in my life and in the lives of those around me. I hope each one who reads these words will do the same. I pray you find Yahweh in every lovely moment, every storm, every time you go around a mountain, and every time you are faced with a giant. May you recognize His great mercy and grace in His story written on the pages of your life.

EPILOGUE

I am days away from publishing this book at the near closing of the year 2017. But before I finalize this book, I want to share an important discovery, made by Terry in the middle of 2017...

I used to chew gum all the time. What I didn't know is that there are three artificial sweeteners in that gum. That 'fake' sugar can cause symptoms that are like multiple sclerosis symptoms! The problem with my legs had gotten to the point where I struggled to walk properly. I eliminated artificial sweeteners and cleansed my body, and many months later, I'm happy to say my legs have been strengthened.

It wasn't until late fall that I finally discovered the cause of the pain and burning in my legs. It was due to damaged, knotted and inflamed Iliotibial (IT) bands in my thighs. Physical therapy, massage, and heat have slowly begun resolving this issue. Praise Yahweh!

I can't say I've solved the great mystery of why things happen the way they do. All I know for certain is Yahweh loves us and He will help us through whatever problems come our way.

Made in the USA
Middletown, DE
27 January 2021